CW00848181

Generative AI for Beginners Made Easy

Master Artificial Intelligence and Machine Learning Fundamentals, Learn Creative AI, and Enhance Your Skills with Interactive Real-World Exercises

ModernMind Publications

Contents

Exclusive Bonus: 200+ ChatGPT Prompts!

Unlock your productivity, save time, and generate income with our FREE bonus for readers of "Generative AI for Beginners Made Easy." This exclusive collection of beginner-friendly ChatGPT prompts is designed to elevate your efficiency, streamline tasks, and explore new opportunities for success.

Why Grab This Bonus?

• Enhance productivity with tailored ChatGPT prompts.

• Save precious time with optimized query strategies.

• Discover innovative ways to earn using generative AI.

Transform your approach to work and creativity with the power of generative AI. This bonus unlocks a world of possibilities for you.

Access the bonus by scanning the QR code below.

Complimentary Audiobook Access

Get the Audiobook version for FREE!

We're pleased to offer the Audible version of our book for free for new Audible users. This promotion provides immediate access to our content at no cost. The audiobook enhances the reading experience with engaging narration, bringing the narrative to life with clarity and depth.

Take advantage of this unique opportunity to enrich your reading experience. Scan the QR below and claim your free copy of the audiobook today.

Introduction

The world is evolving rapidly, and one innovation that stands out for its potential to reshape our world is generative artificial intelligence (AI). Imagine waking up to a world where an intelligent system curates your morning news based on your preferences better than you do or where AI can sift through millions of medical records to offer personalized health advice. This isn't a distant future—it's the reality we're stepping into thanks to the pioneering field of generative AI.

As someone who is passionate about making AI accessible to beginners and those not well-versed in tech, I've dedicated myself to demystifying this field. I firmly believe in the transformative power of AI across various sectors, from healthcare to education, and its capacity to enhance our daily lives in unimaginable ways.

This book is designed to be friendly, encouraging, and optimistic. Its aim is to strip away the layers of intimidation that often shroud AI and present it in a light that is engaging and easy to understand for everyone. The goal is simple: to guide you through the fundamentals of generative AI and its myriad applications and to inspire you to employ AI creatively in real-world scenarios.

Introduction

If you're a beginner or feel overwhelmed by the technical jargon synonymous with AI, this book is for you. It is structured to walk you through the nitty-gritty of AI without getting lost in the complexity. With a structure that unfolds from the basics of AI to its creative applications, complemented by hands-on exercises and illustrative case studies, this book promises a comprehensive learning experience.

Throughout the book, you'll find interactive elements, such as exercises and quizzes, to reinforce your understanding and provide a practical context to the concepts discussed. These components are crucial in bridging the gap between theoretical knowledge and real-world application.

Whether you're looking to enhance your career, ignite your creative passions, or simply gain a deeper understanding of this revolutionary technology, mastering AI opens up a universe of potential.

I invite you to join me on this enlightening journey. I hope you will let the pages of this book inspire you with the endless possibilities that AI offers. With an open mind and a willingness to explore, let's uncover the wonders of AI together. Your guide to navigating the exciting landscape of artificial intelligence awaits. Let's turn the page and begin.

Chapter 1

Decoding Generative AI: Your First Conversation with the Future

In the monotony of our daily lives, lies a silent revolution that is reshaping our interaction with the world. This revolution doesn't have the roar of engines or the clamor of industry, instead it comes with the quiet hum of servers and the soft glow of screens. It's the revolution of artificial intelligence, a field that impacts us all in profound ways. At the heart of this revolution is generative AI, a branch of AI that is not just about understanding the world but about creating new and previously unimagined possibilities.

The ABCs of AI: Understanding the Basics

If you want to delve into the world of generative AI, it's important to start with the basics. Just like building a house requires an understanding of bricks and mortar, exploring AI begins with its fundamental components: AI itself, machine learning, and deep learning. These are not simply buzzwords, but rather the keys to unlocking a deeper understanding of how technology is becoming an integral part of our lives.

Artificial intelligence, in its broadest sense, serves as our modern-day oracle, predicting weather patterns, translating languages in real-time, and even suggesting what series to binge-watch next. Its capabilities are not rooted in magic, but rather in its ability to process and analyze data on a scale that no human could achieve. This is where machine learning comes in, which is a subset of AI that learns from data over time.

Consider how a streaming service might suggest movies that you will enjoy. It's not guesswork, but rather an algorithm that learns from your past viewing preferences, a digital learning process that mirrors how we learn from experience.

Deep learning is a branch of artificial intelligence that uses complex neural networks to process large amounts of data. These networks, inspired by the human brain, can identify patterns and make connections in ways that were once thought to be possible only through human cognition. This technology is used in voice recognition systems that can understand human requests and self-driving cars that can navigate the complexities of the road.

Understanding these concepts can help to demystify the world of AI. Suddenly, the technology that seemed distant and complex becomes more tangible, just like when you first learned how a car engine works or the principles behind the internet. This realization provides a new lens through which to view the world, one where technology's potential is infinte and filled with opportunities for innovation and creativity.

Platforms like Netflix and YouTube use recommendation algorithms that employ machine learning to sift through your viewing history and suggest new content you might enjoy. This is machine learning in action, making your leisure time more enjoyable by personalizing your experience. Similarly, email services like Gmail use machine learning in their spam filters to distinguish between genuine messages and spam, ensuring that your inbox is both manageable and secure.

In these examples, AI, machine learning, and deep learning are not abstract concepts but integral parts of our daily digital experience. They represent the silent orchestrators behind the scenes, making our interactions with technology smoother, more intuitive, and ultimately more human. By understanding these foundational elements, we can see how AI can work for us, opening doors to new possibilities and ways of interacting with the world around us.

Conversations with Machines: How AI Mimics Human Talk

The moment you ask Siri about the weather or interact with a chatbot while shopping online, you're engaging in a sophisticated dance with artificial intelligence. These interactions, often our first foray into the world of AI, peel back the curtain on a technology that, at its core, seeks to understand and replicate human conversation. Chatbots and virtual assistants, from those embedded in retail websites to sophisticated platforms like IBM's Watson Assistant, serve as ambassadors of AI, illustrating its potential to comprehend and cater to our needs.

Imagine logging onto a shopping site, say Shopify, and being greeted by a chatbot ready to assist with your queries. This isn't just a programmed script running predetermined responses but an AI system designed to parse your questions, understand your intent, and provide helpful responses. It's akin to walking into a store and having a conversation with the shopkeeper, except this shopkeeper is digital and powered by algorithms. The ease with which these chatbots blend into our digital interactions speaks volumes about the strides AI has made in understanding human language, making technology feel more accessible and less like an inscrutable black box.

The magic behind these conversational AI systems is Natural Language Processing (NLP). NLP allows computers to break down and interpret human language, turning words and sentences into data that machines can understand and respond to. This technology powers not just chatbots but a plethora of tools that enhance our daily digital experiences. Take Grammarly, for instance, a tool many writers swear by. It uses NLP to scan text for grammatical errors, suggesting corrections and stylistic improvements. What's fascinating is how it goes beyond mere spell-checking, understanding the context of your writing to offer advice that improves clarity and coherence.

Voice-activated devices like Amazon Echo represent another leap in how we interact with AI. Speaking to these devices as we would to another person, we can ask for the news, set reminders, or control smart home appliances. The naturalness of these interactions belies the complex AI algorithms at work, parsing voice commands, understanding intent, and executing tasks. This seamless integration of AI into our homes and lives underscores the shift towards more intuitive technological interfaces, where the line between human and machine interaction blurs.

Yet, as much as NLP has advanced, it's not without its challenges. The complexity of human language, with its idioms, sarcasm, and subtle cues, presents a formidable task for AI. For instance, consider the time I jokingly told Alexa, "We're running low on toilet paper, better order a lifetime supply!" Expecting a witty retort or, at most, a query for clarification, I was astonished to find a mountain of toilet paper at my doorstep the next day. Turns out, Alexa took my hyperbole quite literally, interpreting "a lifetime supply" as an urgent need for 100 packs of toilet paper. This humorous mishap not only gave me a year's worth of anecdotal material but also highlighted the sometimes comical gap between machine understanding and human expression. Strides have been made, and the gap between human and machine communication narrows with each advancement, but perfect understanding remains on the horizon. This ongoing development is a testament to the dynamic nature of AI, constantly evolving and improving in its quest to understand the intricacies of human language.

The emergence of NLP and conversational AI has not only transformed our interactions with technology but also opened up new avenues for innovation. Businesses now harness chatbots for customer service, offering 24/7 support that can handle a multitude of queries simultaneously, improving efficiency and customer satisfaction.

Meanwhile, voice-activated assistants are finding roles beyond personal use, assisting in everything from healthcare to education, where they can provide information, support learning, and even offer companionship.

What stands out in this evolution of AI is its focus on enhancing human interaction rather than replacing it. By automating routine tasks and providing support where needed, AI allows us to focus on the creative and empathetic aspects of our work and lives, enriching our interactions with both technology and each other. The journey of AI, particularly in the realm of NLP, is one of striving to understand and replicate the most human of our abilities—communication. In doing so, it not only makes technology more accessible but also more responsive to our needs, preferences, and nuances.

As we continue to explore the capabilities of AI, particularly its ability to converse and interact with us, it's clear that we're not just programming machines but teaching them to understand and engage with us on a deeply human level. This endeavor, challenging as it may be, holds the promise of a future where technology truly speaks our language, making our interactions with it more natural, intuitive, and, ultimately, more human.

From Sci-Fi to Reality: The Tangible Presence of AI in Daily Life

The impact of AI on our lives has gone from being science fiction to being a reality, and it has happened gracefully. What was once a fantasy, such as self-driving cars and digital assistants, is now a real-world application that is reshaping how we interact with technology.

An excellent example of AI's transformative power is the development of self-driving car technology. Companies like Tesla have integrated AI into automotive navigation with an array of sensors and algorithms that can interpret and respond to the road's nuances in real-time. It's not just about replacing drivers; it's about enhancing safety and efficiency. By reducing human error, which is the leading cause of traffic accidents. These vehicles learn from every trip taken, gathering data to refine their algorithms, which is a continuous process of improvement, similar to human learning curves.

Music streaming services like Spotify use AI to personalize music recommendations. By analyzing your listening habits, such as what songs you play the most, which ones you skip, and the genres you prefer, Spotify's algorithms can curate playlists that feel like they are tailored to your tastes. It's not just about convenience. It also connects you more deeply with music, uncovering new artists and genres you might never have explored otherwise. It shows how AI doesn't just adapt to our preferences, but expands our horizons.

AI's impact extends to healthcare diagnostics, where accuracy is crucial. For example, SkinVision is an app that uses AI to evaluate photos of skin spots and provide users with a risk assessment of skin cancer. This tool empowers individuals with information and access to early detection, potentially saving lives by identifying concerns that warrant a closer examination by medical professionals.

Google's DeepMind has made significant strides in understanding the 3D structures of proteins. This achievement offers hope for treatments for diseases that are currently beyond our grasp. The ability to predict protein structures with precision accelerates the pace of medical research.

Generative AI is a field that showcases an ability to create and innovate. It is not just about understanding or analyzing the world as it is, but about imagining and bringing to life the possibilities of what it could be. It challenges us to think differently about the tools we use, the content we consume, and the methods we employ to tackle some of society's most pressing issues.

The impact of AI on our daily lives is extensive, seeping into facets of our existence in ways we might not even fully appreciate. AI's footprint is expansive, from AI-driven recommendations that influence our shopping decisions to smart home devices that learn our preferences to make our living spaces more comfortable and energy-efficient. It's in the background checks that expedite our travels, the predictive text that speeds up our communication, and the virtual assistants that help organize our days.

Generative AI's emergence into the mainstream is not just about the breadth of its applications, but the depth of its impact. It's reshaping industries, redefining how we interact with technology, and reimagining the limits of what's possible. More than that, it's democratizing access to sophisticated tools and information, leveling the playing field in areas like music production, content creation, and even research.

However, generative AI is still in its nascent stages, with much of its potential untapped. As it continues to evolve, so will its role in our lives, offering new ways to engage with the world, solve problems, and express our creativity. It challenges us to think differently about the tools we use, the content we consume, and the methods we employ to tackle some of society's most pressing issues.

The shift from sci-fi to reality in the context of AI is more than just technological progress; it's a cultural and societal shift towards embracing a future where technology and humanity are increasingly intertwined. This journey into the world of AI, particularly generative AI, invites us to not only witness but actively participate in this unfolding narrative, exploring the myriad ways in which AI can enrich our lives, enhance our capabilities, and elevate our understanding of both the world and ourselves.

Generative AI: The Artistic Side of Algorithms

The realm of generative AI offers a unique intersection of technology and creativity. In this space, algorithms not only solve equations or process data but engage in the act of creation itself. Platforms such as OpenAI's Jukebox are leading the way in this field by using AI to create new musical pieces in various styles. Here, AI goes beyond being just a tool and becomes an artist, composer, and creator, demonstrating how machines can contribute to the world of artistic expression.

Similarly, AI-powered art generators like DeepArt are redefining the boundaries of visual art. By applying algorithms that replicate the styles of well-known painters to photographs, these platforms can turn those that can barely draw stick-figures into artists. Anyone can now create stunning artwork, regardless of whether they have had years of artistic training. AI's potential to democratize creativity and make art more accessible to a wider audience is thus highlighted.

This expansion of creative possibilities challenges the common perception of AI as a purely analytical tool focused on optimization and efficiency. It reveals a side of AI that is imaginative, innovative, and able to contribute to the arts in profound ways. For example, generative AI platforms like ChatGPT are pushing the boundaries of written creativity by providing writers with prompts and suggestions. These AI-powered tools act not only as assistants but as muses, sparking ideas and fostering creativity in poetry and prose. This collaboration between humans and machines opens up new avenues for storytelling, where the AI's suggestions serve as a springboard for the writer's imagination.

The fashion industry is also undergoing a creative revolution due to the integration of AI. Companies such as Stitch Fix are utilizing algorithms to provide personalized clothing recommendations based on individual styles, merging data analysis with fashion sense. This approach goes beyond simple automation, utilizing AI to comprehend and predict fashion trends, customize shopping experiences, and even assist designers in generating new collections. It's a prominent example of how generative AI can impact not just the efficiency but also the very essence of creative industries, offering personalized experiences that reflect individual tastes and preferences.

Apart from these applications, generative AI is also making progress in areas such as game design and architecture, where it helps in developing complex, immersive environments and innovative structures. In game design, AI algorithms can produce unique levels and scenarios, enhancing the gaming experience with infinite variability. In architecture, AI-driven tools assist designers in exploring new forms and structures, pushing the limits of what's architecturally feasible and aesthetically pleasing.

Generative AI has the capability to collaborate with humans in the creative process, which is one of its most compelling aspects. This collaboration is not about replacing human creativity but rather enhancing and extending it. Artists and designers are utilizing AI as a partner in the creative process, leveraging its capabilities to explore new ideas and express themselves in ways that were previously impossible. This partnership exemplifies the potential of AI to act as a catalyst for innovation, encouraging humans to push the limits of their creativity.

Furthermore, generative AI is helping to level the playing field by lowering barriers to entry in various artistic fields. With tools that simplify complex creative processes, more people can participate in artistic endeavors, regardless of their technical skills or background. This democratization is not just about making creation easier but about empowering a broader spectrum of voices and perspectives to contribute to the cultural landscape. It's a shift towards a more inclusive creative world, where diversity of expression is not just welcomed but celebrated.

As generative AI continues to evolve, its impact on the arts and creativity is only set to deepen. With each advancement, we're witnessing a redefinition of what it means to create and who gets to participate in the creative process. This evolution is breaking down the walls between technology and art, revealing a future where AI's role in creativity is as natural and integral as the brush to the canvas or the pen to the page. It's a future where the artistic side of algorithms is embraced for its potential to inspire, innovate, and transform the way we think about art and creativity.

The Everyday AI Toolkit: Practical Tools for the AI Novice

Exploring the world of artificial intelligence doesn't always require complex algorithms or coding skills. In fact, most of us are already using AI in various ways through applications and tools that enhance our daily lives. For those who are interested in AI but unsure of where to start, there are many user-friendly apps available that provide a hands-on experience with the power of AI without requiring any technical background. This section highlights these accessible tools and demonstrates how AI can be a beneficial and practical part of everyday life.

Canva: Unleashing Your Inner Designer

Canva is a graphic design platform that exemplifies the potential of AI in transforming creativity. This platform provides a guiding hand for those who are interested in creating visually appealing content without a background in design. With the help of AI-driven recommendations on layouts, color palettes, and typography, Canva significantly simplifies the design process by removing guesswork. Whether you need to create a poster for a local event or a graphic for your blog, Canva's AI-powered interface helps you select the right elements that work well together, ensuring that the final product is both attractive and professional. By enabling direct interaction with AI-driven design tools, Canva demystifies the technology and showcases its role as a creativity enabler.

Grammarly: More Than a Writing Assistant

Grammarly is a powerful writing tool that goes beyond the standard spell-check functions found in most text editors by using AI technology to improve the quality of writing. It acts as a real-time writing coach, analyzing text for not only spelling and grammar errors but also tone, style, and clarity. Whether you are drafting an email, writing a report, or working on a novel, Grammarly's suggestions can help refine your writing and ensure that your message is conveyed effectively. This tool demonstrates how AI can play a crucial role in communication by offering insights that elevate the quality of the written word. With regular use, even beginners can learn how AI analyzes language and start anticipating suggestions while understanding the reasons behind them.

Photobooth: Capturing Moments with AI

Google's Photobooth app is powered by AI and offers a more intuitive photo-taking experience. It automatically detects when subjects in the frame are ready to be captured, whether they are smiling, making a funny face, or in a candid moment. Users don't need to press a button to take the photo. This application of AI makes our personal experiences more seamless and enjoyable, showing how technology can enhance our lives. It's an example of how AI can anticipate our needs, working in the background to enrich our interactions with the digital world.

Duolingo: Personalized Language Learning

Language learning has been transformed by online platforms such as Duolingo, which uses AI to provide a personalized educational experience. The platform adjusts each lesson according to the learner's pace and progress, ensuring that challenges are customized to their level of skill. Mistakes receive immediate and constructive feedback, similar to the way a personal tutor would provide it, but with the added convenience of being able to learn at any time and from anywhere. This adaptive learning method keeps motivation levels high and makes the process of learning a new language more effective and engaging. For beginners in AI, Duolingo acts as a practical demonstration of how AI can be utilized for personalized education, catering to individual learning styles and requirements.

By using AI-powered applications, we can experience the practical benefits of AI in our daily lives. It helps us enhance our creative projects with Canva, improve our writing with Grammarly, capture moments with Photobooth, and learn languages with Duolingo. These interactions help us to understand how AI works and reveal its potential to enhance personal skills, creativity, and everyday moments. This hands-on approach changes our perception of AI from a complex and distant technology to an accessible and useful tool in various contexts.

Exercise: AI Encounter Journal

Objective: Identify the generative AI technologies you interact with daily to recognize their impact on your routine.

Task: For one day, maintain a journal of your encounters with AI. Note each time you use AI-driven technology, such as navigation apps, recommendation systems, or digital assistants. Reflect on the role of AI in these experiences by answering these questions:

1. How did the AI influence your decision-making or convenience?
2. Identify which interaction felt the most seamlessly integrated into your life and explain why.

Exercise: Design Your Own AI Application

Objective: Apply your understanding of generative AI by conceptualizing an AI tool that enhances your daily life or hobby.

Task: Imagine an AI application that could significantly benefit you personally or professionally. Outline your concept by addressing the following:

1. Define the core function of your AI and the problem it solves.
2. Describe the data it would use and its learning approach to continually improve its service.
3. Envision how users would interact with your AI and the practical benefits they would gain.

Key Takeaways

- **Generative AI Fundamentals:** Grasp generative AI by starting with basic concepts and advancing to its sophisticated applications shaping our future.

- **AI in Everyday Life:** Recognize how generative AI seamlessly integrates into daily routines, powering devices and services we frequently use.
- **Creativity and AI:** Appreciate the creative capacities of AI in art, music, and writing, showcasing its potential beyond analytical tasks.
- **Interactive Understanding:** Enhance comprehension of AI's impact and potential through direct interaction and practical exploration of AI tools.

Chapter 2
Deciphering AI's Alphabet Soup

Staring into the dense fog of AI terminology might feel like you're trying to read a map with no legend. Suddenly, terms like "neural networks" and "algorithm" pop up, making you wonder if you need a degree in computer science just to get started. But here's a secret: stripping AI down to its basics is like learning the rules to your favorite board game. Initially, it seems complex, but soon you're playing with confidence, strategizing, and even enjoying the process. This chapter is your cheat sheet, turning the bewildering array of terms into familiar signposts on your AI exploration.

Sifting Through AI Jargon: Terms You Need to Know

AI doesn't have to be a jumble of intimidating terms; Like learning any new language, start with the basics. Understanding these terms is your first step into the expansive world of AI, a world changing how we live and work.

Artificial Intelligence (AI): Imagine a robot that learns to make your favorite coffee just the way you like it — strong, with a dash of cinnamon. That's AI in a nutshell: a computer system smart enough to learn and adapt to performing tasks, making life a bit easier and more enjoyable.

Generative AI: Think of an artist who creates new, original pieces of art. Generative AI, in a way, is the artist of the AI world. It can generate new content — be it text, images, or music — that has never been seen or heard before, based on its training from existing data. This is the technology behind deepfakes, AI-generated artwork, and new music compositions.

Machine Learning (ML): Now, let's say you teach that coffee-making robot to improve its brewing method based on your reactions (a satisfied sigh or a grimace). ML is the process that allows the robot to refine its coffee-making skills from your feedback without you manually adjusting it each time.

Deep Learning (DL): Consider our robot attending a barista course, learning from thousands of coffee recipes and customer reactions. DL involves layers upon layers of learning (neural networks), enabling the robot to understand complex patterns and make decisions similar to a seasoned barista.

Algorithm: An algorithm in AI is a set of rules or instructions for solving a problem. Think of making your grandmother's famous lasagna. You follow her recipe, a step-by-step guide, to recreate that masterpiece. An algorithm is similar — it's a set of instructions AI follows to complete tasks, from identifying spam emails to recommending a new song.

Data Mining: This is the process of digging through data to find hidden patterns and insights. Picture an enormous library where instead of books, there are bits of data. Data mining is like sending in a detective (your AI) to find the specific information you need — say, the latest trends in coffee drinking habits — hidden within those bits.

Neural Network: Imagine a bustling office where each employee is responsible for a small part of a larger project. They collaborate, passing information back and forth, refining it until the final product emerges. A neural network operates similarly; it's composed of layers of 'neurons' that process input data, learn from it, and communicate with each other to produce an output. This structure is inspired by the human brain, albeit wildly simplified.

Supervised Learning: This concept can be likened to a classroom setting where a student learns under the guidance of a teacher. The teacher (in AI, the dataset you provide) has the answers to the test (the task you want the AI to perform). Through examples and corrections, the student (the AI model) learns to make predictions or decisions based on new data it hasn't seen before.

Unsupervised Learning: Now, imagine a student learning through exploration and curiosity, without a teacher's direct instruction. The student observes the world, identifies patterns, and forms conclusions. In unsupervised learning, the AI system is given data without explicit instructions on what to do with it. The system must find structure in the data on its own, like clustering similar items together.

Reinforcement Learning: Picture training a dog with treats. You reward the behaviors you want to encourage and ignore or correct the ones you don't. Reinforcement learning works on a similar principle; the AI system learns to make decisions by performing actions and receiving feedback in the form of rewards or penalties. It's a trial-and-error learning process aimed at maximizing some notion of cumulative reward.

Machine Vision: Imagine having the ability to scan a crowded room and instantly recognize a friend's face among the strangers. Machine vision gives AI systems a similar capability, enabling them to interpret and understand visual information from the world around them. This technology powers everything from automated quality control in manufacturing to facial recognition systems.

Natural Language Processing (NLP): Remember the thrill of learning to read, gradually making sense of the letters and words until they formed coherent sentences and stories? NLP enables AI systems to 'read' and understand human language, turning text and speech into a form that machines can process and respond to. It's the driving force behind virtual assistants, translation services, and many other applications that require interaction in natural language.

Chatbot: This is your go-to digital assistant, ready to help at any hour. Whether you're asking about the weather or need help with an online purchase, chatbots are AI programs designed to simulate conversation, making digital interactions smoother and more human-like.

Navigating through the AI lexicon isn't just about memorizing terms; it's about seeing the incredible potential these technologies have to transform our world. From the simplicity of getting your morning coffee order just right to the complexity of sifting through massive data for insights, AI is reshaping our daily experiences. This chapter aims to peel back the layers of complexity and showcase AI in a light that's understandable, relatable, and, most importantly, accessible to everyone.

By understanding these fundamental terms, you're better equipped to recognize AI in action, from the mundane to the extraordinary. It's everywhere — optimizing your route to work to avoid traffic, filtering out spam to keep your inbox clean, or even curating personalized playlists that set the mood for your day. AI is not just a technological revolution; it's a tool that, when understood and used wisely, can significantly enhance the quality of our lives.

So, as you progress through this guide, remember that each term you learn, each concept you grasp, brings you one step closer to demystifying AI. It's not about mastering a complex field overnight but about building your understanding one term at a time, much like assembling a puzzle. Each piece is crucial, and with patience and curiosity, the bigger picture of AI's role in our world becomes clearer and more fascinating.

With this foundation, we're ready to explore how to choose the right AI tools and navigate common challenges, ensuring your path through the world of AI is as smooth and rewarding as possible.

Exercise: AI Terminology Crossword Puzzle

Objective: Solidify the understanding of AI jargon by engaging with the terms in a fun, puzzle-solving context.

Instructions:

1. Create a crossword puzzle incorporating key AI terms introduced in the chapter, such as Artificial Intelligence, Machine Learning, Deep Learning, Algorithm, Data Mining, Chatbot, and Computer Vision.
2. Provide definitions or clues related to how these terms are used in the context of AI. For example, the clue for "Algorithm" might be: "A set of rules or instructions in AI that helps solve problems or make decisions."
3. Attempt to solve the puzzle, and then check your understanding by revisiting the section of the chapter where these terms are explained. This will reinforce your memory and understanding of each term.

Choosing Your AI Toolkit: Beginner-Friendly Platforms

In the immense ocean of AI, finding the right tools can feel like searching for a lighthouse to guide your ship safely to shore. The digital landscape offers a plethora of tools, but not all are suited for those just dipping their toes into the AI waters. The key lies in discovering platforms that simplify the complex, turning what might seem like a daunting tech adventure into a delightful journey of discovery and creativity.

Zapier – Automating Tasks With Ease

Imagine having a digital butler, capable of connecting your favorite apps and services, orchestrating them to work together seamlessly. This isn't a peek into a future utopia but a snapshot of what Zapier offers today. With Zapier, the hassle of manual data entry or task management fades into the background, replaced by automated workflows that bridge the gap between disparate applications.

For instance, you might use Zapier's AI to set up a 'Zap' that triggers an automatic email response whenever you receive a new entry in your online form. Simply type in something like "I want to send welcome emails to people that sign up using my online contact form," and Zapier will create a workflow for you. As someone who has spent hours setting up automated workflows before, this can save you hours of frustration.

You can also use Zapier to create chatbots that can help you automate and improve some customer service functions. Customize your chatbot by providing it with specific knowledge (like company documentation) to respond to customer questions, giving it a specific speaking style, and defining its actions. Or perhaps, every time someone books an appointment on your calendar, Zapier could automatically send a reminder SMS an hour before the scheduled time.

The beauty of Zapier lies in its simplicity. With intuitive interfaces and a wide array of pre-built 'Zaps,' you're equipped to automate with confidence, regardless of your technical prowess.

IFTTT (If This Then That) – Crafting Your Digital Recipes

Stepping into the realm of IFTTT is akin to discovering a cookbook for the digital age, where recipes serve not to satiate hunger but to streamline your digital life. IFTTT operates on a simple premise: if one action occurs, then trigger another. It's a digital cause and effect that operates across your online services and devices, creating a web of automation that simplifies routine tasks.

Picture capturing a stunning sunset on your smartphone. With IFTTT, that snapshot could automatically upload to your cloud storage, ensuring it's backed up without a second thought Or, imagine your smart lights dimming as the sun sets, creating the perfect ambiance as you settle in for the evening, all triggered by your location and the day's sunset time.

IFTTT's power lies in its ability to connect actions across different platforms, making technology adapt to your lifestyle instead of the other way around.

Google's Teachable Machine – A Playground for Creativity

Diving into Google's Teachable Machine feels like stepping into a sandbox where the only limit is your imagination. This platform invites you to teach your computer to recognize images, sounds, or even poses, all without writing a single line of code. The process is interactive, engaging, and incredibly informative, offering a hands-on approach to understanding how AI learns from data.

You might train a model to differentiate between pictures of your pets, distinguishing your cat from your dog based on images you provide. Or, perhaps, create a tool that recognizes different gestures, turning physical movements into commands for your computer, like pausing or playing music with a wave of your hand.

Teachable Machine demystifies the learning process of AI, making it accessible and fun, perfect for those eager to see immediate results from their experimentation.

MonkeyLearn – Unveiling Insights Through Text Analysis

MonkeyLearn illuminates the path to understanding the subtleties hidden within text, offering tools that sift through customer feedback, social media comments, or any textual data you wish to explore. This platform embodies the essence of turning data into insight, allowing you to build and use text analysis models with ease.

Envision analyzing customer reviews to gauge overall satisfaction, identifying common praises or points of contention. Or, consider harnessing sentiment analysis to monitor brand perception on social media, turning vast volumes of comments into actionable insights.

MonkeyLearn stands as a beacon for those looking to delve into the nuances of natural language processing, offering a suite of tools that are as powerful as they are user-friendly.

Chatfuel – Simplifying Chatbot Creation

Entering the world of Chatfuel is like unlocking the potential to extend your digital presence around the clock, without the need to scale your team. This platform empowers you to build chatbots for Facebook Messenger, streamlining customer interactions, answering queries, and even processing orders, all automated and efficient

Imagine a chatbot that guides customers through your product catalog, offering personalized recommendations based on their preferences. Or a bot that handles booking appointments, managing schedules directly through Messenger, enhancing customer convenience and satisfaction.

With Chatfuel, the power of conversational AI becomes accessible, transforming how businesses engage with their audience without requiring deep technical knowledge.

Wolfram Alpha – Navigating Complex Queries With Precision

Wolfram Alpha stands as a testament to the power of computational intelligence, offering a tool that goes beyond traditional search. It answers complex queries with precision and insight, from mathematical equations to factual questions about the world. Curious about the stars visible in your location tonight? Wolfram Alpha provides a map of the night sky, tailored to your exact location and time. Wondering about the nutritional content of your lunch? Input your meal, and receive a detailed breakdown of calories, vitamins, and more.

Wolfram Alpha serves as a digital oracle, providing answers that are not just responses but insights, making it an invaluable resource for learners, educators, and the innately curious.

Navigating the AI field with these tools transforms the journey from one of uncertainty to empowerment. Each platform, with its unique offerings, ensures that stepping into AI is not a leap into the unknown but a guided exploration of a world brimming with possibilities. Whether automating tasks, delving into data analysis, or creating interactive AI models, the toolkit available today makes the adventure into AI not just accessible but thoroughly enjoyable.

Exercise: Your AI Toolkit Adventure

Objective: Explore beginner-friendly AI tools to understand their practical applications and get hands-on experience.

Instructions:

1. Choose two AI tools from the chapter, such as Zapier, IFTTT, Google's Teachable Machine, MonkeyLearn, Chatfuel, or Wolfram Alpha.
2. For each tool, go through a simple tutorial or create a basic project. For example, use Teachable Machine to create a model that recognizes different facial expressions, or set up an IFTTT applet that automates a task you do daily.
3. Reflect on the process: What did you learn? How could the tool be useful in your personal or professional life? Write a short summary of your experience and any ideas you have for using these tools in the future.

Navigating the Bumps on the AI Road

Tackling the obstacles in the realm of AI can sometimes feel like trying to solve a puzzle where the pieces keep changing shapes. It's easy to feel stuck or overwhelmed. Yet, with a few practical adjustments and a new perspective, these challenges can transform into stepping stones rather than stumbling blocks.

Error Messages: A Step Towards Clarification

Encountering error messages while experimenting with AI platforms isn't a sign of failure but an invitation to engage more deeply with the problem at hand. Instead of viewing these messages as roadblocks, consider them as clues leading you towards a solution. It's akin to realizing halfway through a recipe that the oven wasn't preheated. The immediate reaction might be frustration, but the solution is straightforward — preheat the oven and proceed. Similarly, when an AI project hits a snag, break down the error message and identify the specific part of the message that pinpoints where things went awry. Then, compare with examples. Sometimes, seeing how others approached similar issues can shed light on your situation.

Documenting Your AI Experiments: The Learning is in the Process

Keeping a detailed record of your AI experiments acts as a navigational tool, guiding you through your exploration of AI. This documentation isn't just a diary but a map of your journey, highlighting both the paths taken and the obstacles encountered. It's the scientific method applied to your AI explorations, where recording each step provides a clear picture of your progress and areas needing adjustment. Reflecting on these notes helps identify patterns in what works and what doesn't, fine-tuning your approach with each project.

Tackling Information Overload: One Bite at a Time

The deep ocean of AI information available can easily lead to a sense of drowning in data, theories, and tools. The antidote to this overwhelm is selective focus. Just as you wouldn't attempt to prepare an entire banquet in one go, diving into AI requires a step-by-step approach. Choose one area of interest or tool and dedicate your efforts to understanding it thoroughly before moving on to the next. Applying this focused learning allows for deeper comprehension and skill mastery, making the process more manageable and enjoyable.

Connecting AI Concepts to the Real World: Bridging Theory and Practice

Understanding AI in abstract terms is one thing; seeing its impact and application in the real world is another. This connection between theory and practice brings AI to life, demonstrating its relevance and potential. To strengthen this link, identify everyday technologies and platforms you use that employ AI, from social media algorithms to smart home devices. Then, analyze how these technologies enhance or simplify your life, providing a practical context to the AI concepts you're learning.

Reaching Out and Experimenting: Building Confidence Through Community and Practice

Embarking on the AI path is not a solitary journey. A wealth of communities and forums exists, populated by individuals at all stages of learning. Engaging with these groups can provide support, answer questions, and offer encouragement. Moreover, embracing experimentation and the inevitable mistakes that come with it is crucial. Each misstep is not a setback but a lesson, refining your understanding and skills. Remember, online forums and communities are invaluable resources, offering insights, advice, and encouragement from those who've navigated similar paths. Additionally, experiment boldly with AI projects, viewing each attempt as a step towards mastery, regardless of the outcome.

In wrapping up, overcoming the hurdles encountered on the AI path is less about finding immediate solutions and more about adopting a mindset of curiosity, resilience, and continuous learning. Each challenge faced is an opportunity for growth, offering insights that refine your understanding and application of AI. This approach not only makes the journey more rewarding but also lays a solid foundation for deeper exploration and innovation in the chapters to come. As we move forward, the focus shifts from navigating challenges to harnessing AI's potential to drive creativity and transformation, opening new avenues for exploration and impact.

Key Takeaways

- **Engage with AI Vocabulary:** Actively familiarize yourself with core AI terminology to navigate the field confidently and communicate effectively.
- **Experiment with AI Tools:** Hands-on exploration of beginner-friendly AI platforms to practically apply your knowledge and enhance your digital proficiency.

- **Incorporate AI into Daily Tasks:** Apply AI concepts to your everyday activities or projects, using AI to streamline processes and improve efficiency.
- **Adopt AI Problem-Solving:** Cultivate a troubleshooting mindset to tackle AI challenges, enhancing your skills through practical resolution strategies.

Chapter 3

The Magic Behind the Curtain: Machine Learning Unveiled

Imagine you're in a kitchen, surrounded by ingredients you've never used before. At first glance, the task of cooking a meal might seem daunting. Yet, with a good recipe and a bit of trial and error, you find yourself whipping up dishes you didn't think were possible. This is akin to the essence of machine learning (ML) - an area of artificial intelligence that, at first, might seem complex but becomes approachable and even intuitive with the right guidance.

Machine learning is the invisible chef in the world of AI, working behind the scenes to make sense of data and improve outcomes over time. It's a dynamic field where algorithms learn from experience, much like refining a recipe with each attempt. This chapter aims to demystify machine learning, breaking it down into digestible concepts, and showcasing its impact on our daily lives.

The Fundamentals of Machine Learning: A Non-Techie's Primer

Machine learning is, at its core, a way for computers to learn from data and improve their performance over time without being programmed for each task. It's like teaching a child to ride a bike; you don't instruct on every pedal push but encourage them to keep going even after they fall. The child learns, adjusts, and eventually rides smoothly. Similarly, ML algorithms improve their decision-making with experience, turning data into insights and actions.

Exploring the Feedback Loop

Think of machine learning as a feedback loop. It starts with an algorithm making predictions or decisions based on data. Then, based on the outcomes of those decisions, the algorithm adjusts, aiming for better accuracy next time. This loop, akin to refining a recipe after each attempt, is what allows machine learning models to improve continually.

Real-World Example: Your Email Spam Filter

A familiar example of machine learning in action is the spam filter in your email. Initially, it might let some spam messages slip through. However, as you mark these as spam, the filter learns and adapts, becoming better at filtering unwanted messages over time. This continuous improvement is machine learning at work, making your inbox cleaner and more relevant without any manual rule-setting by you.

Variety in Learning Styles

Machine learning isn't one-size-fits-all; it adapts to different types of data and objectives through varied learning styles:

- **Supervised Learning**: This style is like learning with a teacher. The model learns from labeled data—it knows the correct answer upfront. It's similar to a student learning history from a textbook that has all the dates and events clearly marked.
- **Unsupervised Learning**: Here, the model learns through observation, finding patterns in the data on its own. Imagine trying to understand the rules of a new board game by watching others play without knowing the instructions beforehand.

- **Reinforcement Learning**: This approach involves learning through trial and error, much like learning to ride a bicycle. The model makes decisions, receives feedback (rewards or penalties), and uses this feedback to make better decisions in the future.

The Learning Journey

Starting with the basics is like distinguishing the melody from background noise. Recognizing the difference between relevant data (signal) and irrelevant data (noise) is crucial. From there, understanding algorithms as sets of rules guiding the learning process, akin to a cookbook for preparing a meal, lays the foundation. It's important to remember that making mistakes, or encountering errors, is a natural part of the learning process. These errors help the model to adjust and improve, similar to how practice helps a musician perfect their tune.

Machine learning, with its feedback loops and varied learning styles, is a testament to how AI systems can grow and adapt. It's a process of continuous improvement, driven by data and experience. Whether it's filtering spam from your inbox or suggesting the next song you might like, machine learning is working quietly in the background, making technology smarter and more intuitive. This chapter aims to peel back the curtain on machine learning, showing it not as a daunting field of study but as an accessible and integral part of the technological advancements that shape our daily lives.

By breaking down these concepts into relatable analogies and everyday examples, the hope is to illuminate the path for anyone curious about machine learning. It's about showing that, with a bit of guidance and curiosity, understanding the magic behind the curtain is not only possible but also incredibly rewarding.

Machine Learning in Daily Life: AI Around Us

The tapestry of our daily lives is interwoven with threads of machine learning, subtly yet significantly altering the fabric of our routine experiences. This evolution from novelty to normalcy showcases the pervasive and practical applications of AI that many might not recognize as machine learning at work.

Language Translation Services: Bridging Worlds

In a bustling café in a foreign land, you pull out your phone, aiming its camera at the menu. Instantly, dishes described in an unfamiliar script transform into your native language, thanks to Google Translate. This app uses machine learning algorithms trained on vast datasets of languages to not only translate words but also grasp context, idioms, and cultural nuances.

Navigation Apps: Steering Through the Fast Lane

Picture this: you're running late for a meeting and your usual route is congested. Waze comes to your rescue, suggesting an alternate route that saves precious minutes. It's a complex dance of machine learning models predicting traffic flow and optimizing routes in real-time, based on historical data and current conditions.

Personal Health and Fitness Apps: Your Digital Coach

Gone are the days of generic workout plans and diet charts. With MyFitnessPal, your smartphone becomes your personal trainer and nutritionist. It customizes workout and meal plans by analyzing your activity levels, dietary preferences, and health goals and adapting as you progress.

Precision Agriculture: Sowing Seeds of Innovation

Venture into the fields with Climate FieldView, where farmers use machine learning tools to analyze soil moisture, nutrient levels, and weather patterns to make informed decisions about planting, watering, and harvesting. This showcases how technology optimizes resource use and boosts yields.

Fashion Forward: Trendsetting with Algorithms

In the dynamic world of fashion, Stitch Fix uses machine learning to predict seasonal trends and personalize style selections. It analyzes social media, search patterns, and sales data to forecast what will be popular, ensuring brands are stocked with desirable items.

Cybersecurity: Shielding Digital Domains

As we navigate the digital age, Darktrace utilizes machine learning to analyze patterns in network traffic, identifying potential threats and protecting against cyber attacks by learning from past incidents, securing our digital interactions.

Smart Appliances: The Comforts of Home

Step into a smarter home with the Nest Thermostat, which learns your temperature preferences and adjusts the environment accordingly, demonstrating how machine learning enhances comfort and energy efficiency through adaptive learning.

Content Creation and Assistance: Revolutionizing Productivity with AI

When drafting reports or creating content, OpenAI's ChatGPT exemplifies the power of AI in streamlining the creative process. Generating drafts, suggesting revisions, and offering insights, this tool transforms content creation, making it more about refining ideas and less about the struggle for words.

Through these examples, machine learning is revealed not as a distant technology but as a present and accessible tool, enhancing our daily lives in myriad ways. Its integration across various domains demonstrates its role as a subtle yet powerful enhancer of our experiences, proving AI's relevance and utility in everyday contexts.

Overcoming AI Anxiety: The Friendly Face of Machine Learning

At first glance, machine learning might seem like a complex labyrinth, filled with mathematical formulas and technical jargon. However, when we strip away the intimidating exterior, we find a field deeply rooted in something quite familiar: the human ability to recognize patterns and learn from them. This realization can transform machine learning from a daunting subject into an accessible and engaging field of study.

Machine learning algorithms are essentially trying to mimic the way humans learn, adapting and improving based on feedback, much like we do. Think of these algorithms as puzzle enthusiasts. Every piece of data is a puzzle piece, and the goal is to fit these pieces together in the most logical way. This perspective makes machine learning more relatable, turning abstract concepts into a problem-solving adventure.

Practical Demonstrations Bring Machine Learning to Life

One of the most compelling ways to illustrate the relevance of machine learning is through its practical applications in our lives. Consider, for instance, how machine learning algorithms are used to filter out background noise in hearing aids. This technology significantly improves the quality of life for its users, allowing them to engage in conversations and enjoy sounds that might otherwise be lost in the noise.

Moreover, machine learning plays a critical role in environmental conservation. By monitoring wildlife populations and analyzing environmental data, algorithms help scientists and conservationists protect endangered species and manage natural resources more effectively. These examples highlight machine learning's global significance, demonstrating its potential to address complex challenges and make a positive impact on the world.

It's Never Too Late to Start Learning

One of the key messages I hope to convey is that it's never too late to start learning about machine learning. Across the globe, individuals from various backgrounds and stages of life are discovering the joy and value of engaging with AI. By sharing success stories of those who have embraced machine learning later in their careers, I aim to inspire and reassure you that embarking on this learning path can lead to rewarding outcomes.

Furthermore, there's a wealth of resources and communities available to support beginners on their machine learning journey. From online courses and tutorials to forums and study groups, the AI community is welcoming and eager to help newcomers find their footing. This abundance of learning materials and the camaraderie among learners create a supportive environment that fosters growth and encourages exploration.

In wrapping up this exploration of machine learning, it's clear that the field is not just about algorithms and data; it's about unlocking new possibilities and understanding the world in novel ways. Machine learning offers tools to enhance our lives, protect our planet, and connect us more deeply with each other. As we move forward, we'll delve into how AI is not only a technological revolution but also a catalyst for creativity and innovation, opening doors to new forms of expression and understanding.

Exercise: Identify the Machine Learning

Objective: To help readers recognize machine learning applications in their daily environment.

Instructions:

1. List down five daily activities or routines (e.g., checking emails, using a GPS navigator, browsing online stores, taking photos, or setting up calendar reminders).
2. Next to each activity, describe how machine learning might be involved in enhancing or facilitating the experience. If unsure, make an educated guess based on the principles learned in this chapter.

Exercise: Machine Learning Styles Role-Play

Objective: To deepen understanding of different learning styles in machine learning through a role-playing exercise.

Instructions:

1. Choose three everyday scenarios (e.g., cooking a new recipe, playing a new video game, or learning to play a musical instrument).
2. For each scenario, decide which type of machine learning (supervised, unsupervised, or reinforcement) best matches the learning process involved in the scenario and explain why.
3. Reflect on how the chosen type of machine learning could mimic the learning process in each scenario, drawing parallels between the AI learning method and human experience.

Key Takeaways

- **Intuitive AI:** Machine learning is a natural, intuitive process, akin to how humans learn from experience.
- **AI in Daily Life:** Machine learning is integral to everyday applications, enhancing everything from email to smart homes.
- **Learning Styles:** Understand the varied learning approaches in AI, including supervised, unsupervised, and reinforcement learning.
- **Demystifying AI:** Overcoming AI anxiety with a clear, relatable understanding of how machine learning works and its positive impacts.

Chapter 4

AI in the Living Room: Making Your Home Smarter

There's a quiet revolution happening right under our noses, and it's taking place in the most familiar of settings: our homes. Gone are the days when the idea of talking to your house seemed like a scene from a science fiction movie. Today, thanks to generative AI, our living spaces are becoming extensions of our digital selves, capable of anticipating our needs, conserving our resources, and even entertaining us in more immersive ways than we ever thought possible.

Smartening Up Your Home With AI

Generative AI: The Architect of Modern Comforts

Using AI to automate and optimize tasks in your home is becoming increasingly accessible. Take the Nest Thermostat, for example, which can learn your temperature preferences and adjust the climate in your home accordingly, factoring in your habits, the weather outside, and the time of day. This helps to ensure maximum comfort while minimizing energy use, making it a great example of thoughtful and intelligent technology.

Similarly, the Roomba Vacuum Cleaner uses AI to map your home, allowing it to clean your floors as efficiently as possible. And with Philips

Hue smart lighting, you can set the perfect ambiance for any occasion, with the lights automatically adjusting to your schedule. These are just a few examples of how AI is making our lives easier and more comfortable.

Easy Setup: No Tech Guru Required

The beauty of these AI-driven devices lies in their simplicity. The era when setting up technology in your home required an engineering degree is behind us. Now, devices boast plug-and-play installation, with user-friendly apps that guide you through the setup process step by step. Many manufacturers provide detailed tutorials, and there's a wealth of how-to videos online that cover everything from unboxing to optimization.

Experiencing AI Firsthand: The Gateway to Curiosity

Starting to use these AI-enhanced devices at home breaks down the wall of apprehension many have about AI's complexity. When you see a Roomba navigating around your living room on its own or your lights dimming just as you're about to start a movie, the magic of AI becomes tangible. It's these everyday interactions that turn skepticism into wonder, sparking a desire to learn more about what AI can do.

Imagine waking up to a home that's already brewing your coffee, adjusting the temperature, and slowly brightening the lights to ease you into the day. Or picture returning from work to find your home perfectly cooled, your favorite playlist streaming through the speakers, and the oven pre-heated, ready for dinner. This isn't a fantasy; it's the reality AI is creating in our homes.

Making Your Space Intuitively Yours

The shift towards smart homes is more than a convenience; it's about crafting spaces that understand and adapt to our needs. The Nest Thermostat, for instance, doesn't just learn your preferred temperatures; it senses when you're away, conserving energy and cutting costs without any input from you. Similarly, Roomba's AI doesn't merely clean; it learns the layout of your space, becoming more efficient with every pass. And Philips

Hue lights can sync with your entertainment system, turning movie night into an immersive experience.

The Ripple Effect of First Encounters with AI

Starting small, with a single device, often leads to a domino effect. As you grow comfortable and see the benefits, integrating more AI into your home feels like the next natural step. Each device added weaves a tighter mesh of smart technology, transforming your living space into a finely tuned environment that reflects your habits, preferences, and even moods.

Embracing AI, Step-by-Step

For those hesitant about diving into AI, starting with smart home devices provides a gentle introduction. It's an opportunity to experience the practical benefits of AI firsthand in a context that's both familiar and controlled. As comfort with these technologies grows, so too does the curiosity to explore further, opening doors to deeper understanding and more sophisticated applications of AI.

Incorporating AI into our homes is just the beginning. As we become more familiar with its capabilities, the possibilities for enhancing our daily lives expand exponentially. From creating more efficient living spaces to personalizing our environments in ways we've yet to imagine, AI holds the key to a future where our homes are not just places we live but spaces that live with us.

Exercise: AI Smart Home Challenge

Objective: Experience the practicality of AI in everyday living by conceptualizing a smart home setup using generative AI technologies.

Instructions:

1. Pick three rooms in your home (e.g., kitchen, living room, bedroom).
2. For each room, identify one task or routine you'd like to automate or enhance with AI (e.g., adjusting temperature, optimizing

lighting, cleaning).

3. Outline a plan detailing which AI-powered devices (like a smart thermostat, AI vacuum cleaner, or smart lighting) you could use, how they would integrate into your daily routine, and the benefits you'd expect.
4. Reflect on how these changes could improve energy efficiency, convenience, or personalization in your living space.

Exercise: Interactive Guide to Setting Up Your Smart Home

Objective: Gain hands-on experience in integrating AI technology into your home by setting up your first smart device, enhancing your living space with the convenience and efficiency of AI.

Instructions:

1. **Select Your Device:** Choose a basic AI-powered smart home device to start with, such as a smart thermostat, a smart light bulb, or a smart plug. Ensure the device is compatible with your home setup and has an accompanying app for control.
2. **Unboxing and Setup:** Carefully unbox the device, keeping all manuals and accessories handy. Locate the setup instructions either in the manual provided or on the manufacturer's website.
3. **Installation:** Follow the step-by-step instructions for installing the device. This might involve physical installation (like screwing in a smart light bulb) and technical setup (like connecting the device to your home Wi-Fi network).
4. **App Configuration:** Download the corresponding app on your smartphone or tablet. Create an account if required, and pair the device with the app following the on-screen instructions. This step is crucial for enabling smart features and remote control.
5. **Customization:** Explore the app to customize the device settings. Set up schedules, adjust preferences, and explore different modes (e.g., eco-mode on a thermostat, color settings on a light bulb, or timing schedules for a smart plug).

6. **Integration Testing:** Test the device thoroughly to ensure it's working as expected. Adjust the settings, and monitor the device's response to ensure it meets your needs and preferences.

7. **Optimization Tips:** Look for additional features in the app that can enhance your experience, such as energy-saving tips, maintenance notifications, or firmware updates to keep the device functioning optimally.

8. **Reflection:** Reflect on how the device could change your daily routine, increase energy efficiency, or provide convenience. Consider how you might expand your smart home ecosystem with additional devices in the future.

AI as Your Personal Finance Advisor

Navigating the waters of personal finance often feels like trying to decode a map without a compass. The good news? AI has stepped in as a reliable navigator, making financial management not just simpler but also surprisingly insightful. It's as if you have a financial advisor in your pocket, one that's attuned to your habits, goals, and preferences.

Transforming Budgeting with a Digital Touch

Apps have become the new age financial diaries, logging every transaction, categorizing expenses, and even highlighting patterns we might overlook. Imagine an app like YNAB (You Need A Budget), which does more than just track your spending. It analyzes your transactions, categorizes them into neat buckets, and even nudges you when you're about to overspend on takeout coffee. This isn't just tracking; it's understanding and advising, powered by AI that learns from your financial behavior to offer tailored budgeting advice.

Every transaction you make is logged and analyzed, giving you a live view of your financial health. You can opt to get notifications for unusual spending or when you're nearing budget limits, keeping you on track without the need for manual checks. You can also see your spending habits broken down into colorful charts, making it easier to spot areas for adjustment.

Investment Guidance Tailored for You

For those venturing into the investment world, platforms like Betterment serve as an automated guide, simplifying the complexities of stock markets and portfolios. Using algorithms, these platforms manage your investments, aligning them with your risk tolerance and financial goals. It's like having a personal investment manager who's always always optimizing your portfolio. Here are some benefits of using an automated investment platform:

- **Automated Portfolio Management**: Your investments are continuously monitored and adjusted based on market trends and your personal goals.
- **Risk Assessment**: Algorithms evaluate your risk tolerance, ensuring your investments match your comfort level.
- **Effortless Diversification**: Spread your investments across a wide range of assets automatically, reducing risk and improving potential returns.

Robo-Advisors: Keeping Your Goals in Sight

The term "robo-advisor" may bring to mind a cold and impersonal machine, but in reality, these AI-powered advisors are designed to help you stay on track with your long-term financial goals. They constantly rebalance your portfolio, keeping you aligned with your investment objectives even during market fluctuations. Robo-advisors use a proactive approach to investing that puts your goals first. They keep you informed about your progress towards financial milestones and make necessary adjustments to keep you on course. They also employ tax-efficient strategies like tax-loss harvesting to minimize your tax liabilities and maximize your investment growth.

Demystifying Finance with Clarity and Insight

simplify complex ideas into practical, easy-to-follow insights. For individuals lacking a financial background, this is a game-changing tool. These AI-powered tools not only provide recommendations, but also educate users by presenting the abstract concepts of personal finance in a more concrete and understandable way. In order to make financial recommendations more comprehensible, these tools provide clear and straightforward explanations. Additionally, visual representations, such as charts and graphs, help users better understand financial trends and the consequences of their financial decisions.

A Less Daunting Financial Environment

Budgeting and investing can be overwhelming tasks, but with AI as your financial companion, they become more approachable. The constant feedback and personalized advice help you to approach your finances more informed and engaged. It's like having a financial coach by your side, always looking out for your best interest and guiding you towards sound financial health.

You'll receive proactive tips tailored to your unique situation so that you can improve your financial habits. Regular updates on your financial status keep you connected and motivated, turning passive tracking into active management. In this age of information, AI stands out as a beacon of simplicity and insight, making financial planning and investing accessible to all.

With AI as your guide, the path to financial stability and growth becomes clearer and more attainable. You'll open up a world where managing your money is not a chore but an empowering part of everyday life.

Exercise: AI Financial Advisor Simulation

Objective: Simulate the experience of using an AI-powered financial tool to understand how it can assist in managing personal finances.

Instructions:

1. Create a fictional monthly budget including income, expenses, savings, and investments.
2. Use the principles of AI financial tools (like budget tracking, investment advising, or transaction alerts) to analyze your budget. You can do this manually or use a generic financial planning app to get a feel for the process.
3. Develop a strategy for how you would adjust your spending, savings, and investments based on the AI-generated insights and recommendations.
4. Journal the potential long-term benefits and challenges you foresee with relying on AI for personal financial management.

Cultivating Your Green Thumb with AI

In the realm of backyard botany and urban farming, a quiet revolution is underway, powered by generative AI. This movement is transforming novices into green-fingered enthusiasts, enabling lush gardens and bountiful harvests through the magic of technology. The entry point into this verdant world is more accessible than ever, thanks to smart gardening systems and AI-driven applications designed to demystify the complexities of plant care.

Imagine a device, small yet powerful, discreetly nestled in your garden soil. This is the Edyn Garden Sensor, a sentinel in your quest for gardening excellence. It continuously monitors environmental conditions, analyzing moisture levels, sunlight exposure, and nutrient composition. This data, once the exclusive domain of seasoned horticulturists, is now readily available, providing you with real-time insights and actionable advice tailored specifically to your garden's needs.

AI Plant Diagnosis Apps

Photographs have the power to capture beauty, but in the hands of a gardener, they can also diagnose and heal. AI-powered apps like Plant AI have emerged as modern-day plant doctors, capable of identifying diseases and pest infestations with a quick snapshot. Within moments, you're equipped with a diagnosis and a treatment plan, turning potential disasters into minor setbacks easily overcome.

Automated Watering Systems

Water is life, especially in the garden. Yet, too little or too much can spell disaster for your plants. Automated watering systems, guided by AI, take the guesswork out of hydration. These systems learn the optimal watering schedule for your garden, factoring in weather forecasts, soil conditions, and plant requirements. The result is a perfectly watered garden with minimal waste, ensuring each plant receives just the right amount of care.

Demystifying Gardening

For those who've admired lush gardens from afar, convinced that a green thumb was out of reach, AI offers a bridge to gardening success. The technology peels back the layers of horticultural mystery, presenting gardening as a series of logical steps supported by data. Suddenly, what seemed like an arcane art becomes a manageable, even enjoyable, endeavor. With AI by your side, every step from seedling to harvest is informed, intentional, and infinitely more likely to succeed.

Sustainability and Connection

Beyond the personal joy and satisfaction that comes from nurturing a garden, AI-driven gardening aligns with broader environmental goals. It champions sustainable living, encouraging more people to grow their own food, reduce waste, and understand the delicate interplay between nature and nurture. This approach not only yields healthier plants and more abundant harvests but also fosters a deeper connection with the environment, highlighting the role technology can play in promoting a greener, more sustainable world.

The impact of AI in gardening extends beyond individual success. It's about collective empowerment, enabling communities to grow more with less, share knowledge, and support one another in their horticultural endeavors. The technology invites a reevaluation of how we interact with our environment, suggesting a path where balance and abundance go hand in hand.

In this green journey, AI stands as a beacon, illuminating the path to gardening success. It offers a helping hand to those just starting, a wealth of knowledge for the curious, and a vision of a more sustainable future for all. The promise of generative AI in gardening is not just about the gardens we grow but about the kind of world we cultivate around us.

As we close this chapter on AI's role in personal and environmental growth, we're reminded of the broader implications of this technology. It's a tool that, when used wisely, has the potential to transform not just our personal spaces but the planet as a whole. This exploration of AI's impact on our homes, finances, and gardens serves as a foundation for the next steps in our journey. It invites us to consider how AI can not only enhance our lives but also address some of the most pressing challenges we face as a global community.

Exercise: Virtual AI Gardening Project

Objective: Explore the impact of AI in gardening and agriculture by planning a virtual garden with AI assistance.

Instructions:

- Choose a type of garden you'd like to cultivate (e.g., vegetable, flower, herb).
- Research and select an AI gardening tool or app that could help in managing your garden, such as soil sensors or plant disease identifiers.
- Virtually plan your garden, deciding what plants to grow based on AI recommendations for soil conditions, climate, and disease prevention.
- Create a maintenance schedule using AI predictions for watering, fertilizing, and harvesting, and reflect on how this technology

could make gardening more efficient and successful.

Key Takeaways

- **Embrace Smart Living:** Integrate AI devices like smart thermostats and lighting into your home to enhance comfort, efficiency, and convenience.
- **Optimize Finances with AI:** Utilize AI-powered financial tools to analyze spending, optimize investments, and receive personalized budgeting advice.
- **Green Your Thumb with AI:** Employ AI in gardening to monitor plant health, optimize watering schedules, and get tailored care tips for a thriving garden.
- **Explore AI's Practicality:** Actively engage with AI technologies in everyday scenarios to discover their practical benefits and ease of use firsthand.

Chapter 5

Data at Your Fingertips: AI Tools for Career Advancement

The world is awash in data, from the constant stream of social media updates to the endless arrays of business metrics. In this sea of information, the ability to not just navigate but to make sense of data stands out as a critical skill. It's no longer the exclusive domain of data scientists or IT specialists. Today, with the right tools and a bit of guidance, anyone can learn to harness the power of data to unlock new opportunities and insights.

Climbing the Data Ladder

AI Tools That Turn Data Into Stepping Stones for Career Growth

Navigating through data can feel like trying to scale a mountain. It's daunting at first, but with the right equipment, reaching the peak becomes not just possible but inevitable. Tools like Microsoft Power BI and Tableau act as your gear, transforming raw data into visual stories that highlight trends, patterns, and insights. These platforms democratize data analysis, making it accessible to anyone eager to learn.

Microsoft Power BI: This tool brings data to life, turning complex metrics into interactive dashboards that anyone can understand and use.

Imagine tracking your company's sales performance, visualizing uptrends or downtrends, and identifying opportunities for growth, all with a few clicks.

Tableau: It offers a canvas for your data, allowing you to paint a picture of your business environment. With Tableau, complex datasets become comprehensive visualizations, making it easier to share insights across teams and departments.

By mastering these platforms, you not only add valuable skills to your resume but also gain the ability to uncover insights that can drive business strategies. LinkedIn's 2020 Emerging Jobs Report underscores the growing demand for data literacy across industries, highlighting it as a skill that can significantly boost your career prospects.

Asking the Right Questions of Data

Knowing what questions to ask is as crucial as having the answers. Tools like Google's BigQuery equip you with the ability to query large datasets, honing your analytical skills. It's not just about finding answers but understanding the why and how behind the data.

- Practice with Public Datasets: Google's BigQuery offers access to public datasets, providing a sandbox for you to explore, question, and analyze. This hands-on experience is invaluable, teaching you not just how to navigate data but to extract meaningful insights that inform decisions.
- Impress in Job Interviews: Demonstrating a grasp of data analytics tools and the ability to derive insights from datasets can set you apart. It shows initiative and a proactive approach to problem-solving, traits highly valued in any role.

Understanding Customer Behavior Through AI Analytics

Platforms like Hootsuite Insights and Sprout Social leverage AI to sift through social media trends, offering a window into customer behaviors and preferences. For anyone in sales or marketing, these insights are gold, enabling targeted strategies that resonate with your audience.

- **Hootsuite Insights**: Imagine being able to listen to what your customers are saying across social media platforms in real-time. Insights gathered can shape your marketing strategies, ensuring your messages hit the mark.
- **Sprout Social**: It goes beyond listening, offering analytics that track engagement and performance across channels. This feedback loop allows you to refine your approach continuously, ensuring your social media efforts contribute positively to your brand's reputation and bottom line.

Leveraging these insights can directly impact sales and marketing performance, elevating your role within the team and the broader organization. It's about making informed decisions that not only respond to current trends but anticipate future ones.

Data literacy is no longer a nice-to-have; it's a must-have in today's job market. With tools like the ones discussed in this section, the power to understand and utilize data is at your fingertips. Whether you're looking to shift into a data-centric role or simply enhance your current skill set, the ability to interpret and leverage data can open doors to new opportunities and insights, positioning you for success in an increasingly data-driven world.

Exercise: Data Visualization Challenge

Objective: Utilize AI tools to transform raw data into compelling visual insights, enhancing your data literacy and storytelling skills.

Instructions:

1. **Select a Dataset:** Choose a public dataset from platforms like Google's BigQuery or any open-source data repository. Pick a dataset relevant to your interest or industry.

2. **Explore AI Tools:** Use AI-powered data visualization tools like Microsoft Power BI or Tableau. Familiarize yourself with the basics through introductory tutorials if you're a beginner.
3. **Create Visualizations:** Develop a series of visualizations that reveal interesting trends, patterns, or insights from the dataset. Experiment with different chart types and formats to best represent the data.
4. **Interpret Your Findings:** Write a brief report summarizing the key insights from your visualizations. Explain how these insights can inform business strategies or decisions.
5. **Present Your Work:** Share your visualizations and findings with peers or mentors, and gather feedback on your analysis and presentation skills.

Streamlining Project Management with AI

In the dynamic world of project management, where deadlines loom and tasks pile up, AI has emerged as a beacon of efficiency. It's transforming traditional methods, making project oversight more intuitive and less time-consuming. Tools like Asana and Trello are at the forefront of this shift, incorporating AI to automate and prioritize tasks, thereby simplifying project management even for those just starting out in this field.

Making Project Management More Intuitive

For anyone who has ever felt overwhelmed by the intricacies of managing a project, AI-driven tools like Asana and Trello offer a sigh of relief. These platforms harness AI to streamline task prioritization and forecast project timelines, effectively taking the guesswork out of project management.

- **Automating Routine Tasks**: Begin by automating simple, repetitive tasks. This not only saves time but also introduces you to the capabilities of AI in a manageable way.
- **Predicting Project Timelines**: With AI, these tools can forecast how long tasks will take to complete. This insight allows for more

accurate planning and resource allocation, ensuring projects stay on track.

The beauty of starting small with AI is that it builds your confidence. As you become more comfortable with automating tasks, the door opens to tackling more complex project management challenges. It's a step-by-step process that gradually enhances your skills and understanding of AI's potential in project oversight.

Keeping Teams in Sync with AI

In today's world, where remote work has become the norm, maintaining team cohesion across distances is crucial. This is where AI-powered collaboration tools like Slack come into play. They ensure that information flows smoothly within the team, keeping everyone aligned and focused.

- **Managing Information Flow**: Slack utilizes AI to filter and direct information, ensuring team members only receive notifications relevant to their work. This keeps everyone from being overwhelmed by unnecessary details and helps maintain focus on their tasks.
- **Facilitating Seamless Collaboration**: The ability to integrate with other AI-driven project management tools means that Slack can act as a central hub for all project communications, making it easier for teams to collaborate effectively, regardless of their physical location.

Getting to know these collaborative tools can make you an invaluable asset to any remote team. It shows that you're not just capable of surviving in modern work environments but thriving in them.

Enhancing Decision-Making with AI

Every project comes with its set of risks and uncertainties. Anticipating these challenges and preparing for them is where AI truly shines. Tools like nTask use AI to offer insights into potential project hurdles before they become issues, allowing for proactive problem-solving.

- **Risk Assessment and Management**: By analyzing data from previous projects, AI can identify patterns and predict potential risks, giving project managers the foresight needed to mitigate them effectively.
- **Preparation and Problem-Solving**: Armed with predictive insights, you can develop strategies and contingency plans, showcasing your ability to tackle challenges head-on. This not only keeps projects on track but also demonstrates valuable problem-solving skills to employers.

The integration of AI into project management doesn't just streamline workflows or enhance collaboration; it redefines what it means to lead projects in the digital age. It equips you with the tools to anticipate challenges, make informed decisions, and drive projects to successful completion.

Navigating the project management scenery with AI by your side transforms an often daunting task into an exciting opportunity to innovate and excel. Whether automating routine tasks, keeping teams connected, or anticipating project risks, AI empowers you to tackle the complexities of project management with confidence. It's an invitation to explore the potential of AI in redefining project success, paving the way for more efficient, effective, and collaborative work environments.

Exercise: AI-Enhanced Project Management Simulation

Objective: Implement AI-driven project management tools to streamline workflow, improve efficiency, and enhance team collaboration.

Instructions:

1. **Scenario Creation:** Outline a hypothetical project relevant to your field, including goals, timelines, tasks, and team roles.

2. **Tool Selection:** Choose an AI-enhanced project management tool like Asana or Trello. Set up a project space and familiarize yourself with its AI features, such as task automation, deadline predictions, or workflow optimizations.

3. **Simulation Exercise:** Simulate the project execution using the tool, incorporating AI features to assign tasks, set deadlines, and monitor progress. Use the tool's collaboration features to simulate team updates and communication.

4. **Evaluate AI Impact:** Reflect on how the AI features affected the project management process. Consider aspects like time saved, ease of collaboration, and the accuracy of AI predictions.

5. **Feedback Loop:** Discuss your experience and the tool's effectiveness in a group or with a mentor, focusing on how AI can enhance project management practices.

Becoming an AI-Savvy Marketer

In the ever-evolving topography of digital marketing, the fusion of creativity with the analytical prowess of AI is reshaping strategies and narratives. This blend not only refines the way brands connect with their audiences but also opens up a playground of opportunities for those ready to dive into the nuances of AI-driven marketing.

Personalization at Scale

At the heart of modern marketing lies the promise of personalization - the ability to tailor experiences and messages to the individual at scale. AI-driven tools like HubSpot and Salesforce are redefining this promise, turning oceans of customer data into detailed maps of preferences, behaviors, and needs.

- **HubSpot** shines by offering marketers the tools to segment audiences with precision, delivering content and campaigns that resonate on a personal level. Imagine sending out a marketing email that addresses each recipient by name, references their past interactions with your brand, and recommends products based on their purchase history.

- **Salesforce**, on the other hand, excels in creating a 360-degree view of the customer, enabling marketers to anticipate needs and craft campaigns that feel less like broadsides and more like conversations. This capability ensures that every touchpoint, from social media to customer service, is informed by a deep understanding of the customer's journey.

For beginners stepping into the realm of digital marketing, grasping these AI-powered segmentation tools is like finding a compass. It guides your efforts, ensuring that your marketing strategies are not just seen but felt, fostering connections that drive engagement and conversion.

The Art of AI-Driven Content Creation

In a world where content is king, the ability to consistently produce material that is both relevant and engaging is a Herculean task. Enter AI-driven platforms like MarketMuse, which arm marketers with insights to elevate their content strategy.

- **MarketMuse** offers a window into the mechanics of content performance, analyzing gaps in your material and suggesting improvements. It's akin to having a seasoned editor at your side, one who not only spots weaknesses but recommends specific fixes, from keyword inclusion to topical depth.
- This technology transforms the content creation process, enabling even those who don't consider themselves writers to produce work that stands out. It's not just about making content that's good enough; it's about pushing boundaries and setting new standards in engagement and value.

Adopting these content optimization tools sets you apart as a marketer. It shows you're not just playing the game but changing it, crafting messages that not only reach audiences but resonate with them on a deeper level.

Insights That Drive Strategy

The true power of AI in marketing lies in its ability to turn data into insights and insights into action. Tools like AdEspresso by Hootsuite offer a glimpse into this transformative potential, providing granular analytics on campaign performance that inform smarter, more effective strategies.

- **AdEspresso** simplifies the complexity of online advertising, giving marketers a clear view of what works and what doesn't. With this tool, the effectiveness of each ad, from the imagery used to the copy written, is measured and analyzed, offering a playbook for optimization that is constantly updated.
- For someone just beginning their journey in digital marketing, the ability to interpret and act on these insights is a game-changer. It's not about making educated guesses but informed decisions that amplify the impact of every marketing dollar spent.

Embracing these AI tools equips you with a level of insight typically reserved for seasoned professionals. It empowers you to fine-tune campaigns in real-time, ensuring that your marketing efforts are not just seen but felt, driving engagement, and fostering connections that matter.

In the dynamic field of digital marketing, AI is not just a tool but a partner. It offers a path to personalization at a scale previously unimaginable, elevates content creation beyond mere craftsmanship to an art form, and turns data into actionable insights that sharpen strategy. For those ready to explore this synergy, the opportunities are boundless, promising a journey not just of career advancement but of transformation.

Exercise: Crafting AI-Powered Marketing Campaigns

Objective: Leverage AI-driven marketing tools to develop personalized marketing strategies and content, boosting engagement and conversion rates.

Instructions:

1. **Campaign Conceptualization:** Devise a brief outline for a marketing campaign, including target audience, key messages, and desired outcomes.
2. **Utilize AI Tools:** Employ AI tools like HubSpot or MarketMuse to analyze customer data, generate content ideas, and optimize your marketing messages.
3. **Develop Content:** Create a range of marketing materials (e.g., email campaigns, social media posts, blog articles) using AI suggestions for personalization and relevance.
4. **Analyze Campaign Performance:** Use AI analytics tools, such as AdEspresso, to simulate the monitoring of your campaign's performance, adjusting strategies based on AI-generated insights.
5. **Reflect on Learnings:** Assess the effectiveness of your AI-enhanced approach and document the potential benefits and challenges you encountered, focusing on how AI can transform marketing efficiency and impact.

Mastering Customer Service with Conversational AI

In an era where immediacy reigns supreme, conversational AI has transformed customer service, introducing a new era of efficiency and personalization. This transformation is marked by the emergence of AI chatbots and virtual assistants, tools that not only offer round-the-clock support but also ensure human resources are reserved for more complex customer queries.

Platforms like Dialogflow and Drift have made it possible for businesses, regardless of size, to deploy responsive customer service bots. These bots are capable of managing a high volume of inquiries, from tracking orders to answering frequently asked questions, freeing up human agents to handle more nuanced conversations. For individuals stepping into customer support roles, becoming proficient in setting up and managing these systems opens doors to new career opportunities, positioning you as a forward-thinking professional in a tech-driven landscape.

But the magic of conversational AI doesn't stop at handling inquiries. Tools like Chattermill leverage machine learning to distill actionable insights from customer feedback, providing a holistic view of customer sentiment across various channels. This data-driven approach to understanding customer needs and pain points is invaluable for businesses aiming to elevate their service quality and, by extension, customer satisfaction. For those new to customer service, harnessing these insights can lead to significant improvements in service delivery, earning recognition for proactive management and strategic thinking.

Moreover, conversational AI has revolutionized the way businesses approach sales and recommendations. Much like the personalized suggestions offered by platforms like Netflix, AI algorithms in chatbots can tailor product recommendations to individual customers, enhancing the shopping experience and boosting sales metrics. This level of personalization not only increases customer satisfaction but also drives revenue growth, creating a win-win scenario for businesses and consumers alike. For beginners in retail or e-commerce, mastering the use of conversational AI for personalized sales can set you apart, showcasing your ability to leverage technology to drive business success.

The integration of conversational AI into customer service is not just about technology; it's about reimagining the customer experience. By ensuring inquiries are managed efficiently, insights from customer interactions are utilized to improve service, and sales are boosted through personalized recommendations, businesses can foster stronger relationships with their customers. For those at the start of their career, embracing these tools means stepping into a role where you can make a tangible impact, using technology to enhance the way businesses connect with their clients.

As we wrap up this exploration of conversational AI in customer service, it's clear that the journey into the world of AI is filled with opportunities to innovate and improve business practices. From setting up chatbots that streamline customer inquiries to analyzing feedback for actionable insights and personalizing sales strategies, the potential for impact is immense. For beginners, navigating this environment offers a chance to not only develop new skills but also to contribute to shaping the future of customer service. As we move forward, the focus shifts to looking beyond individual tools and towards understanding the broader implications of AI on business and society, inviting an ongoing dialogue about the ethical and practical considerations of these technologies.

Key Takeaways

- **Leverage AI for Data Insights:** Utilize AI-powered data analysis tools to uncover valuable business insights, enhancing your decision-making and strategic thinking skills.
- **Streamline with AI Project Management:** Adopt AI-driven project management software to optimize workflow, increase efficiency, and foster effective team collaboration.
- **Enhance Marketing with AI:** Employ AI tools to personalize marketing efforts, create targeted content, and analyze campaign effectiveness, thereby improving engagement and ROI.
- **Innovate Customer Service:** Integrate conversational AI into customer service to provide instant, reliable support and gain insights into customer preferences and satisfaction.

Chapter 6

The Entrepreneur's AI Toolkit: Transforming Business with Smart Technology

In today's fast-paced market, staying ahead isn't just about keeping pace; it's about setting the tempo. Entrepreneurs now have a powerful ally in this endeavor: artificial intelligence. This chapter shines a light on how AI tools offer a crystal ball into market trends, customer preferences, and competitive terrains, providing the insights needed to make informed, strategic decisions.

AI-Driven Market Insights

Navigating the intimidating sea of market data can feel like trying to find a treasure without a map. Fortunately, AI tools have emerged as the compass entrepreneurs need, quickly analyzing data to reveal the X marks the spot for business opportunities.

Platforms Like Crayon Track Competitor Website Changes

Imagine waking up to an email alert that your main competitor has launched a new product overnight. With platforms like Crayon, this isn't just possible; it's a daily reality. Crayon monitors changes across competitor websites, alerting you to updates in real-time. This means you're always in the loop, able to adjust your strategies with agility, ensuring your business stays one step ahead.

Google Analytics for Audience Segmentation and Prediction

Google Analytics goes beyond counting website visits; it's like having a conversation with your customers without them saying a word. By segmenting audiences and predicting future actions, this tool lets small business owners tailor their marketing efforts with precision, ensuring messages reach the right eyes and ears at the right time.

Real-Time Feedback with Brand24

In a world where brand perception can shift overnight, staying informed is paramount. Tools like Brand24 serve as the ears on the ground, providing real-time feedback on how your brand is perceived across social media and the web. This immediate insight allows for swift, informed decisions, turning potential crises into opportunities for engagement and growth.

Predictive Analytics to Forecast Market Demands

When it comes to allocating resources, guessing games can be costly. Enter predictive analytics. IBM's SPSS Statistics software and platforms like InsideSales offer a peek into the future, using data-driven models to anticipate customer behaviors and market trends. This foresight is invaluable, helping entrepreneurs allocate resources wisely and stay ahead of market demands.

Benchmarking with Owler and SEMrush

Knowing where you stand in the market is crucial. Owler delivers competitor insights directly to your inbox, painting a clear picture of your industry standing. Meanwhile, SEMrush's Market Explorer offers a panoramic view of your market, from audience demographics to seasonal trends. Together, they provide a 360-degree view of where you stand and where the opportunities lie.

Case Study 1: FashionSync – Boutique Retailer's AI-Enhanced Forecasting Model

Background: "FashionSync," a boutique retailer renowned for its distinctive fashion selections, encountered the challenge of keeping pace with rapidly shifting fashion trends. They sought a sophisticated method to predict upcoming trends accurately and align their inventory to meet consumer demands effectively.

Strategy: FashionSync adopted an AI-driven predictive analytics approach, similar to IBM's SPSS Statistics, integrating a variety of data inputs such as historical sales, fashion industry trends, and social media insights to forecast future fashion trends and customer preferences.

Implementation:

- **Data Integration:** Merged retrospective sales data with contemporary insights from fashion trend reports and social media trends.
- **Predictive Analysis:** Utilized AI algorithms to process the integrated data, providing forecasts on upcoming fashion preferences and potential sales trends.
- **Inventory Strategy:** Adjusted their stock procurement and inventory levels in line with the AI-generated forecasts, ensuring readiness to meet market demand.

Outcomes:

- **Enhanced Sales Performance:** FashionSync saw a notable increase in sales, attributed to their strategic alignment of product offerings with the AI-driven trend forecasts.
- **Inventory Optimization:** Achieved a significant reduction in surplus inventory, minimizing waste and optimizing warehousing costs through informed stock management.

- **Improved Customer Satisfaction:** Enhanced customer experiences by ensuring high-demand trends were readily available, leading to higher customer retention and loyalty.

Lessons Learned:

- AI-powered trend forecasting can profoundly influence inventory management and sales strategies, ensuring retailers remain competitive and responsive to market dynamics.
- Integrating diverse data sources into AI models can enhance the accuracy of predictions, providing a solid basis for business strategy adjustments.
- Continuous refinement and calibration of AI models are essential to adapt to the ever-evolving fashion industry, ensuring sustained business growth and relevance.

Case Study 2: Market Pulse – Tech Startup's Competitive Edge with Real-Time AI Monitoring

Background: "TechInnovate," a startup specializing in smart home devices, needed to navigate a highly competitive market and differentiate itself from larger incumbents.

Strategy: The company employed a tool like Crayon to monitor competitors' online activities, tracking updates on websites, product launches, and customer feedback across the industry in real time.

Implementation:

- **Competitor Analysis:** Utilized AI to continuously scan and analyze competitors' websites and social media for new product announcements, pricing changes, and customer reviews.
- **Agile Marketing:** Adapted marketing campaigns and product development swiftly in response to the insights gained from the AI tool, ensuring relevancy and competitiveness.

- **Strategic Alerts:** Set up real-time alerts for specific triggers, such as competitor product launches or significant changes in online sentiment.

Outcomes:

- **Proactive Strategy Adjustments:** Rapidly adjusted business strategies in response to the AI-generated insights, staying ahead of competitors.
- **Market Share Growth:** Enhanced market responsiveness led to a 15% increase in market share as they capitalized on emerging opportunities quickly.
- **Informed Product Development:** Integrated customer and competitor insights into the product development process, resulting in highly competitive and innovative products.

Lessons Learned:

- Continuous monitoring of the competitive landscape with AI tools can provide a significant advantage in rapidly evolving markets.
- Real-time insights allow for agile decision-making, ensuring that marketing and product development efforts are always one step ahead.
- Understanding the broader market context through AI not only informs strategic decisions but also drives tangible business growth and innovation.

Checklist: AI Market Insight Tools

This checklist is a handy guide for entrepreneurs to evaluate which AI tools best fit their business needs, including key features to look for and questions to ask providers.

AI MARKET INSIGHT TOOLS
checklist

☐ **DATA INTEGRATION CAPABILITIES:**

  ☐ CAN THE TOOL SEAMLESSLY INTEGRATE WITH YOUR EXISTING DATA SOURCES AND PLATFORMS?

  ☐ DOES IT SUPPORT VARIOUS DATA FORMATS AND LARGE DATASETS?

☐ **REAL-TIME ANALYTICS:**

  ☐ DOES THE TOOL PROVIDE REAL-TIME DATA ANALYSIS AND INSIGHTS?

  ☐ HOW QUICKLY CAN IT PROCESS NEW DATA AND UPDATE ITS OUTPUTS?

☐ **PREDICTIVE ANALYTICS:**

  ☐ CAN THE TOOL FORECAST FUTURE MARKET TRENDS BASED ON HISTORICAL DATA?

  ☐ DOES IT OFFER ACTIONABLE INSIGHTS FOR DECISION-MAKING?

☐ **USER-FRIENDLY INTERFACE:**

  ☐ IS THE DASHBOARD INTUITIVE AND EASY TO NAVIGATE FOR USERS WITHOUT TECHNICAL EXPERTISE?

  ☐ ARE THERE CUSTOMIZABLE OPTIONS TO TAILOR THE INTERFACE TO YOUR BUSINESS NEEDS?

☐ **SCALABILITY:**

  ☐ CAN THE TOOL SCALE UP TO ACCOMMODATE GROWING DATA NEEDS AND COMPLEXITY?

  ☐ IS IT FLEXIBLE ENOUGH TO ADAPT TO YOUR BUSINESS'S EVOLVING REQUIREMENTS?

☐ **COMPLIANCE AND SECURITY:**

  ☐ DOES THE TOOL COMPLY WITH RELEVANT DATA PROTECTION REGULATIONS (E.G., GDPR)?

  ☐ WHAT SECURITY MEASURES ARE IN PLACE TO PROTECT YOUR DATA?

☐ **SUPPORT AND TRAINING:**

  ☐ DOES THE PROVIDER OFFER ADEQUATE TRAINING AND RESOURCES TO HELP YOU MAXIMIZE THE TOOL'S UTILITY?

  ☐ IS THERE RELIABLE CUSTOMER SUPPORT AVAILABLE FOR TROUBLESHOOTING AND GUIDANCE?

AI MARKET INSIGHT TOOLS
checklist (cont.)

QUESTIONS TO ASK PROVIDERS:

☐ **CUSTOMIZATION AND FLEXIBILITY:**
  ☐ HOW CUSTOMIZABLE IS THE TOOL IN TERMS OF FEATURES, REPORTING, AND DATA ANALYSIS?
  ☐ CAN IT BE TAILORED TO SPECIFIC INDUSTRIES OR BUSINESS SIZES?

☐ **INTEGRATION WITH OTHER TOOLS:**
  ☐ HOW WELL DOES IT INTEGRATE WITH OTHER TOOLS AND SYSTEMS YOU ARE CURRENTLY USING?
  ☐ IS THERE AN API FOR CUSTOM INTEGRATIONS?

☐ **COST AND PRICING STRUCTURE:**
  ☐ WHAT IS THE PRICING MODEL, AND HOW DOES IT SCALE WITH USAGE OR OVER TIME?
  ☐ ARE THERE ANY HIDDEN COSTS OR POTENTIAL FEES FOR ADDITIONAL SERVICES?

☐ **SUCCESS STORIES AND CASE STUDIES:**
  ☐ CAN THE PROVIDER SHARE SUCCESSFUL CASE STUDIES OR TESTIMONIALS FROM BUSINESSES SIMILAR TO YOURS?
  ☐ HOW HAVE OTHER COMPANIES BENEFITED FROM USING THIS TOOL?

☐ **FUTURE DEVELOPMENTS:**
  ☐ HOW IS THE TOOL EXPECTED TO EVOLVE, AND WHAT NEW FEATURES ARE PLANNED FOR FUTURE RELEASES?
  ☐ HOW DOES THE PROVIDER STAY AHEAD OF EMERGING MARKET TRENDS AND TECHNOLOGICAL ADVANCEMENTS?

☐ **TRIAL AND EVALUATION:**
  ☐ IS THERE A FREE TRIAL OR DEMO AVAILABLE TO EVALUATE THE TOOL BEFORE COMMITTING?
  ☐ WHAT ARE THE TERMS AND CONDITIONS OF THE TRIAL PERIOD, AND WHAT LEVEL OF ACCESS IS PROVIDED?

ModernMind Publications

Navigating the market with AI doesn't just level the playing field; it offers a vantage point previously out of reach for many entrepreneurs. By harnessing these tools, small business owners can glean insights that inform smarter, strategic decisions. Whether it's staying informed about competitors, understanding customer behaviors, or predicting market trends, AI provides the clarity and foresight needed to navigate the complex business world with confidence.

Exercise: AI Market Analysis Simulation

Objective: Practice using AI tools to analyze market trends and consumer behavior, enhancing your strategic marketing insights.

Instructions:

1. **Research AI Tools:** Explore AI-driven tools like Google Analytics or Crayon. Choose a tool that provides market insights or competitor analysis functionalities.
2. **Simulate a Market Study:** Create a hypothetical product or service. Use your chosen AI tool to analyze the market, identifying trends, consumer preferences, and competitor strategies relevant to your offering.
3. **Develop Insights:** Based on the AI-generated data, draft a strategic marketing plan that addresses identified consumer needs, positions against competitors, and leverages market opportunities.
4. **Reflect and Discuss:** Summarize the key insights gained from the simulation and how they could influence real-world business decisions. Share your findings in a discussion group or with a mentor.

Enhancing Customer Experience with AI

Creating memorable connections with customers is at the heart of every successful business. In a setting where personal touch can differentiate a brand, artificial intelligence is stepping in to transform the customer experience into something truly remarkable. This section peels back the layers on how AI is redefining customer engagement, making every interaction not just a transaction but a moment of genuine connection.

Tailoring Interactions with Precision

Imagine if every email you sent felt like a warm handshake, every recommendation like a thoughtful gift. This is the reality AI brings to personalized marketing campaigns, turning every outreach into an opportunity to deepen customer relationships. Services like Mailchimp are pioneering this approach, using AI to ensure that your messages reach the inbox at the perfect moment, filled with content that speaks directly to the recipient's interests and needs.

Optimized Send Times: Mailchimp's AI analyzes user behavior to pinpoint the ideal time for sending emails, ensuring they're opened and read, not lost in the shuffle.

Content Personalization: It goes further by tailoring the email content, making every message resonate on a personal level, significantly lifting engagement rates.

On platforms like Etsy, AI is weaving its magic by guiding users through a marketplace bustling with options, leading them directly to products they'll love. It's like having a personal shopping assistant who knows your taste better than you do, making every visit a discovery of delights perfectly aligned with your preferences.

Personalized Recommendations: Etsy uses AI to curate product suggestions, transforming browsing into a curated experience, elevating user satisfaction and driving sales.

Instant Support, Anytime, Anywhere

In a world that never sleeps, customer queries and issues arise round the clock. Here, AI-powered chatbots and virtual assistants are becoming indispensable allies for businesses, offering instant support without the overhead of a 24/7 customer service team. Tools like ManyChat streamline interactions on platforms such as Facebook Messenger, turning each conversation into an opportunity to impress and assist.

Automated Customer Service: With ManyChat, businesses can create bots that handle a wide array of inquiries, from FAQs to order tracking, ensuring customers always have the support they need.

Virtual assistant services like x.ai take the hassle out of scheduling, coordinating meetings through email and Slack as effortlessly as a seasoned personal assistant. This leaves entrepreneurs free to focus on what matters most, secure in the knowledge that their schedule is in expert hands.

Seamless Scheduling: x.ai simplifies meeting coordination, finding the ideal time for all parties and adding appointments to calendars without the back-and-forth that usually accompanies scheduling.

Listening and Adapting with AI

Understanding customer feedback is crucial, but sifting through comments across platforms can be daunting. Sentiment analysis tools like Lexalytics are turning this challenge into an opportunity. They process immense volumes of text to gauge customer sentiment and offer clear insights into their satisfaction and concerns.

In-depth Sentiment Analysis: Lexalytics examines feedback from various sources, providing a comprehensive view of customer sentiment, helping businesses adapt and improve their offerings.

Platforms such as Qualtrics take this a step further by not just collecting but analyzing survey responses, turning raw data into actionable insights. This feedback loop is invaluable, allowing businesses to fine-tune their strategies and offerings based on direct input from their audience.

Actionable Feedback Insights: Qualtrics uses AI to analyze survey data, highlighting areas for improvement and opportunities to enhance the customer experience.

Through these AI-powered tools, businesses are not only meeting expectations but exceeding them, turning every interaction into an opportunity to impress, engage, and connect. Whether it's through personalized outreach that feels genuinely thoughtful, instant support that resolves issues swiftly, or listening and adapting to feedback with care, AI is setting a new standard for customer experience. In this new era, every touchpoint is an opportunity to build lasting relationships, fostering loyalty and trust that goes beyond the transactional. With AI, businesses are not just selling products or services; they're creating experiences that resonate, endure, and inspire.

Exercise: Personalized Customer Experience Plan

Objective: Design a personalized customer engagement strategy using AI-powered tools to enhance customer satisfaction and loyalty.

Instructions:

1. **Select an AI Tool:** Choose an AI-enabled platform like Mailchimp or Etsy that specializes in personalizing customer interactions.
2. **Craft a Campaign:** Develop a campaign aimed at boosting customer engagement for your hypothetical or existing product/service. Utilize the AI tool to segment your audience, personalize messages, and optimize engagement times.
3. **Analyze the Outcomes:** Imagine the potential outcomes based on the tool's predictive capabilities. Evaluate how personalization could lead to increased customer loyalty or sales.
4. **Evaluate and Iterate:** Reflect on the strategy's effectiveness and areas for improvement. Consider how you would test, measure, and iterate on your campaign in a real-world scenario.

Streamlining Operations with AI

In the bustling world of entrepreneurship, every second counts. The secret to keeping the gears of business turning smoothly often lies in optimizing the mundane—those routine tasks that, while small on their own, collectively consume extensive swathes of time. Here, artificial intelligence emerges not just as a tool but as a transformative force, reshaping business operations.

Zapier: Connecting Apps for Seamless Workflows

Automation platforms like Zapier have redefined efficiency, creating seamless connections between different applications. Picture this: your social media posts, customer inquiries, and even invoice management are all operating in perfect harmony, without the need for constant manual oversight. This symphony of automation liberates entrepreneurs, granting them the freedom to channel their energy towards the creative and strategic initiatives that truly require a human touch.

With Zapier, the once cumbersome task of ensuring your CRM, email, and project management tools work together is simplified. Imagine setting up a process where new customer inquiries from your website automatically populate your CRM and trigger a personalized welcome email. This level of automation streamlines customer engagement and ensures no opportunity falls through the cracks.

Quickbooks: Reducing Errors in Financial Management

QuickBooks, with its AI-driven approach to bookkeeping, stands as a guardian against the all-too-common human errors that can creep into financial management. By automating tasks like expense tracking and invoicing, QuickBooks not only saves time but also introduces a layer of precision that manual processes struggle to match.

The magic of QuickBooks lies in its meticulous attention to detail. Each transaction is recorded and categorized with a level of accuracy that manual bookkeeping can seldom achieve. This ensures your financial records are always up-to-date and reliable, providing a solid foundation for making informed business decisions.

Brightpearl: Optimizing Inventory with AI

On the inventory front, systems like Brightpearl are revolutionizing the way businesses manage their stock. By predicting stock requirements, these AI-powered platforms help prevent overstocking or stockouts, ensuring that you always have the right amount of product at the right time. This not only optimizes inventory levels but also significantly reduces waste and lost sales opportunities.

Brightpearl does more than track stock levels; it anticipates them. By analyzing sales trends, seasonality, and even supplier lead times, it provides recommendations on when to reorder and how much, turning inventory management from a guessing game into a strategic operation.

Lokad: Tailored Demand Forecasting

Demand forecasting tools like Lokad take this a step further, offering tailored optimization for businesses across sectors. Whether you're in e-commerce, manufacturing, or retail, having an accurate forecast of demand means you can better plan your procurement, production, and sales strategies.

Lokad's approach to demand forecasting is both granular and comprehensive. It looks at historical data, market trends, and even external factors like economic indicators to predict future demand. This allows businesses to plan more effectively, ensuring they're ready to meet their customers' needs without tying up unnecessary capital in excess inventory.

Monday.com: AI-Powered Project Management

When it comes to coordinating projects and teams, AI-driven tools are setting new standards for efficiency and collaboration. Monday.com, for instance, uses AI to provide realistic project timelines, helping managers allocate resources more effectively and keep projects on track.

With Monday.com, project managers get a clear view of each project's timeline, including potential bottlenecks and their implications. This foresight allows for proactive adjustments, ensuring that projects meet their deadlines without sacrificing quality.

Jira: Enhancing Team Collaboration with AI

Jira Software harnesses AI to enhance team collaboration, suggesting the best team member for a task based on their workload and skill set. This ensures tasks are allocated not just based on availability but on the optimal match between the task requirements and the team member's expertise.

Jira's intelligent task assignment goes beyond simple delegation. It considers the complexity of tasks, the skills required, and the current workload of each team member. This leads to more balanced work distribution, higher team morale, and, ultimately, better project outcomes.

The integration of AI into business operations is akin to having a silent partner, one that tirelessly works in the background to ensure everything from customer interactions to inventory management runs without a hitch. This partnership not only elevates operational efficiency but also frees entrepreneurs to direct their focus where it matters most: innovating, strategizing, and steering their businesses toward new horizons.

Exercise: Streamlining Your Operations with AI

Objective: Explore how AI can automate operational tasks, saving time and resources for more strategic activities.

Instructions:

1. **Identify Operational Needs:** List down repetitive tasks or processes in your current or hypothetical business that could be automated (e.g., invoicing, email responses, social media posts).
2. **Explore AI Tools:** Research and select an AI tool like Zapier or QuickBooks that can automate these tasks. Understand the features and capabilities of the tool.

3. **Create an Automation Workflow:** Design a workflow that automates a specific task using the chosen tool. Set up the workflow, ensuring it responds to the needs you've identified.
4. **Assess the Impact:** Reflect on how automating this task could improve efficiency, accuracy, and overall business performance. Consider how you could scale this solution to other areas of your business.

AI for Competitive Analysis and Strategic Planning

In the arena of modern entrepreneurship, understanding the environment in which your business operates is not just beneficial; it's pivotal. The strategic use of AI in competitive analysis peels back the layers of your market, revealing not just where you stand but also where the untapped opportunities lie. This clarity is invaluable, equipping you with the insights needed to navigate your business toward growth and innovation.

Kompyte for Real-Time Competitive Intelligence

Imagine having a bird's eye view of your competitors' strategies as they unfold. Kompyte transforms this into reality by tracking competitors' online maneuvers in real-time. This platform acts like a radar, detecting shifts in competitors' strategies, from pricing adjustments to new product launches. With this wealth of information, you're not just reacting to market changes; you're anticipating them, ensuring your strategies are always a step ahead.

- **Spotting Opportunities and Threats**: By understanding competitors' moves, you can identify gaps in their strategies, offering a chance to fill those spaces with your innovative solutions.

Ahrefs for SEO Insights

In the digital age, visibility is currency. Ahrefs serves as a powerful telescope, zooming in on competitors' search traffic to unveil the keywords drawing audiences to their sites. This insight is golden, guiding you in refining your content strategy and keyword optimization to enhance your online presence.

Tailoring your content to include keywords with high traffic but low competition can significantly improve your site's visibility and engagement.

Strategic business planning is also being reshaped by AI, turning what once was a gamble into a calculated move with higher chances of success.

LivePlan for Financial Forecasting

Navigating the financial aspects of business planning can feel like trying to sail in a storm. LivePlan introduces calm, with forecasting tools that predict financial outcomes with impressive accuracy. This foresight aids in risk assessment, ensuring that your business decisions are informed and prudent.

Armed with forecasts, you can make budgetary decisions that sustain growth while avoiding financial pitfalls.

WhatIf for Exploring Business Strategies

The future is not a single path but a web of possibilities. WhatIf stands as your guide through this maze, allowing you to simulate various business strategies and their potential outcomes. This tool empowers you to make choices not on gut feeling alone but backed by data-driven projections.

By exploring different scenarios, you can choose strategies that align with both your short-term objectives and long-term vision.

The tapestry of business management and growth is woven with data. AI-enabled real-time analytics provide a lens to view your business's performance in vivid detail, ensuring that your decisions are timely and based on the latest information.

Sisense for Business Intelligence

In the swirling dance of numbers and metrics that encapsulate your business's health, Sisense acts as a beacon. It integrates data from various sources into a coherent dashboard, presenting a clear picture of where your business stands at any moment.

This real-time overview allows for swift adjustments to strategies, ensuring your business remains responsive and resilient.

Microsoft Azure for Turning Data into Actionable Insights

The cloud-based services of Microsoft Azure bring AI's capabilities right to your fingertips. By turning complex data sets into understandable and actionable insights, Azure ensures that every decision you make is grounded in solid data.

Leveraging Azure's AI capabilities allows you to identify trends and opportunities for innovation, driving your business toward sustained growth.

In navigating the competitive landscape and planning for the future, AI is not just a tool but a navigator, spotlighting the opportunities and challenges that lie ahead. It equips entrepreneurs with the insights necessary to make strategic decisions, ensuring their businesses are not only surviving but thriving in the ever-evolving market. This strategic application of AI paves the way for businesses to not just compete but to lead, setting new standards and opening new frontiers.

As we wrap up, it's clear that the strategic use of AI in competitive analysis and planning is transforming the entrepreneurial setting. From gaining real-time insights into competitors' strategies with Kompyte to exploring future scenarios with WhatIf, AI equips businesses with the tools needed to navigate with confidence. These technologies ensure that every step taken is informed by data, turning potential risks into well-calculated moves. As we move forward, the focus shifts to the broader implications of AI in shaping the future of business, inviting us to consider not just how we can leverage these tools for success, but how they redefine what success looks like in the digital age.

Exercise: Competitive Analysis with AI

Objective: Leverage AI tools to conduct a competitive analysis, identifying opportunities and threats in your business.

Instructions:

1. **Choose a Competitive Intelligence Tool:** Select an AI-powered tool like Ahrefs or Kompyte that can provide insights into your competitors' online strategies.
2. **Analyze Competitors:** Use the tool to gather data on a few main competitors, focusing on their SEO strategies, content, and online presence.
3. **Strategic Insights:** Based on the analysis, identify potential gaps in the market that your business could exploit and areas where your competitors are excelling.
4. **Action Plan:** Develop a brief action plan outlining how you could adjust your business strategies based on your competitive analysis findings.

Key Takeaways

- **Utilize AI for Market Insights:** Harness AI tools to analyze market data, identify trends, and gain a competitive edge by understanding consumer preferences and market dynamics.
- **Personalize Customer Experiences:** Implement AI-driven personalization in your marketing strategies to enhance customer engagement, loyalty, and sales.

- **Automate to Innovate:** Leverage AI to automate routine business operations, allowing you to focus on strategic growth and innovation.
- **Embrace AI for Strategic Decisions:** Use AI-powered competitive analysis and strategic planning tools to make informed business decisions, identify market opportunities, and stay ahead of industry trends.

Chapter 7

The Art of Possibility: Unleashing Creativity with Generative AI

Imagine sitting in front of a blank canvas with an array of brushes, yet no physical paint in sight. Instead, with a few clicks and adjustments on a screen, vibrant landscapes and intricate portraits come to life, guided by the invisible hand of artificial intelligence. This isn't a scene from a futuristic novel; it's the reality of today's creative backdrop, where generative AI is reshaping the boundaries of artistic expression.

In a similar vein, musical composition, traditionally requiring mastery over instruments and an in-depth understanding of theory, is now accessible to anyone with a passion for melodies, thanks to generative AI. This shift not only expands the horizons of what's possible for seasoned artists but also opens the door for novices to step into the realm of music creation with confidence.

The Symphony of AI: Composing Music with Algorithms

Generative AI is transforming the music industry, offering a new way for creators to craft soundscapes. Platforms like Amper Music and AIVA are at the forefront of this revolution, providing tools that allow users to produce music by specifying genres, moods, and even the types of instruments they prefer. These platforms draw from extensive databases of music to learn patterns and craft original compositions, highlighting the potential for AI to be a co-creator in the musical process.

Amper Music and AIVA empower users to create music by adjusting simple parameters, making music composition accessible to all. The technology behind these platforms analyzes vast collections of music to identify patterns and generate new compositions, showcasing the creative potential of AI.

Case Study: Taryn Southern's "I AM AI"

Taryn Southern's album "I AM AI" stands as a testament to the power of generative AI in music. It marks a milestone as the first LP entirely composed and produced with the help of AI, offering a glimpse into the future of music production. This breakthrough demonstrates not only the capability of AI to create commercially viable music but also its potential to become an integral part of the creative process for artists worldwide.

"I AM AI" serves as a real-world example of how artists can leverage AI to push the boundaries of music composition. Southern's collaboration with AI challenges traditional notions of music creation, emphasizing the role of AI as a partner in the artistic process.

Generative AI is democratizing music production, leveling the playing field for those without formal training or access to expensive instruments. With user-friendly interfaces, platforms like Amper Music and AIVA encourage experimentation, allowing users to tweak settings and instantly hear the results. This ease of use opens up a world of musical exploration for hobbyists and aspiring musicians, making the process of creating music more inclusive.

User-friendly interfaces on AI music platforms simplify the composition process, inviting more people to explore music creation. The technology enables individuals to experiment with different sounds and styles, fostering a more inclusive and diverse musical scene.

As generative AI continues to weave its way into the fabric of music production, it also sparks conversations about copyright, authorship, and creativity. The emergence of AI-composed music raises questions about the ownership of creative works and the role of AI in the artistic process. These discussions are vital as they shape the evolving relationship between technology and art, ensuring that the contributions of AI are recognized without diminishing the value of human creativity.

The copyrightability of AI-composed music is a growing area of debate, highlighting the need for clear guidelines on authorship and ownership. Dialogue around the ethical use of AI in music underscores the importance of establishing norms that honor both human and machine contributions to the creative process.

Generative AI is not just a tool for automating the music creation process; it's a catalyst for innovation, enabling artists and enthusiasts to explore new realms of sound. By democratizing access to music production and fostering collaboration between humans and machines, generative AI is redefining musical expression. This shift towards a more inclusive and experimental approach to music opens up a world of possibilities, inviting everyone to experience the joy of creation and the thrill of innovation.

Exercise: AI Music Composition Workshop

Objective: Experience the collaborative process of creating music with AI, exploring the intersection of technology and artistry.

Instructions:

1. **Explore AI Music Tools:** Choose a generative AI music platform like Amper Music or AIVA. Familiarize yourself with its features and capabilities.
2. **Set Your Parameters:** Define the genre, mood, and any other available parameters that will guide the AI in composing your piece.

3. **Collaborate and Create:** Interact with the AI to compose a piece of music. Adjust settings and inputs based on the initial outputs to refine the composition.
4. **Review and Reflect:** Evaluate the final piece. Consider the creative process, how the AI contributed, and how the result aligns with your artistic vision. Share your experience and the piece, if possible, with others.

Brush Strokes & Pixel Plots: AI in Visual Arts

In the realm of visual arts, a fascinating transformation is underway, reshaping the canvas of creativity for both seasoned artists and those just dipping their toes into artistic waters. Here, generative AI emerges not merely as a tool but as a muse and collaborator, expanding the spectrum of creative expression and challenging our very notions of artistry.

Google's DeepDream stands out as a pioneer in this space, blurring the lines between technology and art. By interpreting and enhancing patterns within photographs, DeepDream produces images that are both surreal and mesmerizing, offering us a window into how AI perceives and reimagines the world around us. This project not only pushes the boundaries of visual creativity but also invites us to ponder the potential of AI as an independent creative entity.

The accessibility of art creation has seen a significant leap forward with platforms like RunwayML. Here, the barrier to entry for creating complex visuals is dramatically lowered, allowing anyone with a vision to bring it to life, sans the need for extensive technical know-how. RunwayML democratizes the process of art creation, making it possible for a wider audience to explore and experiment with digital art forms.

Refik Anadol's work exemplifies how AI can bridge the digital and physical realms to create immersive experiences. By harnessing data and AI, Anadol crafts visual experiences that not only captivate the senses but also provoke thought about the interplay between technology and human perception. His installations serve as beacons, illuminating the potential of AI to enrich and expand the horizons of artistic expression.

The emergence of AI art generators has sparked a vibrant debate about creativity, authorship, and the essence of art. Competitions witnessing AI-generated pieces like "Edmond de Belamy" clinching awards have intensified this discourse. This development prompts a critical examination of the value attributed to the human touch in art versus the algorithmic precision offered by AI. It challenges preconceived notions of creativity and prompts us to consider a future where AI plays a central role in artistic creation.

This shift also raises practical questions about the valuation of art in the age of AI. As pieces created by AI begin to enter auctions and command significant prices, they disrupt traditional art valuation models, prompting a reevaluation of what we consider valuable and why. This trend not only opens new avenues for artists to collaborate with AI but also for newcomers to make their mark in the art world. The blending of human creativity with AI's capabilities suggests a future where art is more accessible, diverse, and dynamic.

The discourse surrounding AI and creativity extends beyond the confines of traditional art spaces, influencing how art is taught, experienced, and appreciated. Educational institutions are beginning to integrate AI into their curricula, preparing the next generation of artists for a reality where technology and creativity intersect in unprecedented ways. Museums and galleries are exploring new formats for showcasing AI art, offering visitors interactive and personalized experiences that redefine the act of engaging with art.

Online platforms and social media have become vibrant hubs for sharing and discovering AI-generated art, fostering a global community of creators and enthusiasts. This digital ecosystem encourages collaboration across borders, disciplines, and cultures, driving innovation and experimentation in the visual arts. It highlights the power of AI to not only transform individual artistic practices but also to weave a richer, more interconnected tapestry of global creativity.

The evolution of AI in the visual arts is a testament to the endless possibilities that emerge when technology meets creativity. It challenges us to expand our definitions of art and artist, to embrace the unknown, and to explore the untapped potential at the intersection of human imagination and machine intelligence. In this new era of artistic exploration, AI stands not as a replacement for human creativity but as a catalyst, a tool, and a collaborator, propelling us toward a future where art is more inclusive, innovative, and boundless than ever before.

Exercise: Generative AI Art Challenge

Objective: Utilize generative AI to create unique visual art, pushing the boundaries of traditional and digital artistic expression.

Instructions:

1. **Select an AI Art Generator:** Use a tool like DeepDream or RunwayML that transforms inputs into artistic pieces using AI.
2. **Input and Experiment:** Provide the AI with initial inputs, such as base images or style preferences, and explore the different artistic outputs generated.
3. **Curate Your Gallery:** Select a series of generated images that you feel best represent your creative goals. Consider how the AI interpreted your inputs and the surprises or challenges encountered.
4. **Discuss and Debate:** Reflect on the creative process and the role of AI in your artwork. Engage in discussions about the implications of AI in art, considering questions of authorship, creativity, and the future of art.

Characters and Conflicts: Writing Stories with Generative AI

In the quietly bustling corners of the literary world, a transformation is unfolding, one that sees the pen being passed, at times, from the writer's hand to the circuitry of the AI. Tools like Sudowrite and ShortlyAI are emerging as the unsung heroes for writers at every stage of their journey, offering a wellspring of inspiration for plot twists, character depths, and even entire narratives that might have otherwise lain dormant in the writer's imagination.

The Writer's New Companion

With the advent of Sudowrite and ShortlyAI, the age-old battle against writer's block is taking a promising turn. These platforms serve as a modern-day muse, suggesting not just words but whole worlds, characters with their quirks, and plots with their twists. They operate on a simple yet profound premise: the expanse of literature they've analyzed enables them to suggest content that doesn't just fit the context but enhances the narrative in ways previously unimagined.

Sudowrite and ShortlyAI breathe life into stories, offering suggestions that resonate with the tone and trajectory of the narrative. Their algorithmic analysis of literature equips them to provide contextually relevant and stylistically harmonious suggestions.

The Story of Robin Sloan and Shelley

The narrative of Robin Sloan and his AI collaborator, Shelley, presents a compelling case study of AI's role in the creative writing process. Sloan's use of Shelley to draft narratives demonstrates a harmonious blend of human creativity and machine intelligence, where the AI serves not to dictate but to inspire, suggesting directions that Sloan might not have explored on his own.

Robin Sloan's collaboration with Shelley highlights AI's potential to enrich the writing process while preserving the author's voice. This partnership between human and AI in storytelling underscores the technology's role as a facilitator of creativity rather than a replacement.

Redefining Creativity and Authorship

The emergence of AI-assisted writing sparks a pivotal dialogue on the essence of creativity and originality in literature. The debate centers around the authenticity of stories co-created with AI, challenging us to reconsider our definitions of authorship and creativity. This conversation is vital, nudging the literary world towards a broader acceptance of AI as an instrument of creative amplification.

The discourse on AI-assisted writing encourages a reevaluation of what constitutes originality and creativity in storytelling. It positions AI as a catalyst for creativity, expanding the writer's toolkit rather than diminishing the human element.

A New Era of Storytelling

The innovation doesn't stop at AI-assisted writing; generative AI is also carving out new platforms for storytelling. Interactive fiction platforms like AI Dungeon are pioneering a form of narrative that is dynamically shaped by the reader's choices, blurring the lines between author, reader, and AI. This interactive form of storytelling is not just a novel entertainment medium; it represents a seismic shift in how stories are conceived, created, and consumed.

Platforms like AI Dungeon use AI to craft stories that evolve based on reader input, offering a unique, personalized experience. This interactive storytelling introduces a novel concept, where the narrative journey is co-created by the AI, author, and reader.

These developments in AI-assisted writing and interactive storytelling are not mere technological feats; they are the harbingers of a literary renaissance where the boundaries of creativity are continually expanded. They invite writers to explore uncharted territories in narrative construction, character development, and reader engagement, enriching the tapestry of literature with new textures and hues.

As we close this exploration of generative AI in storytelling, we're reminded of its transformative impact not only on how stories are written but on the very fabric of narrative possibility. From offering a beacon of inspiration in the daunting face of writer's block to crafting dynamic tales that adapt to each reader's journey, AI is redefining literature. This chapter is a testament to the symbiotic relationship between human creativity and machine intelligence, a partnership that promises to usher in a new era of storytelling imbued with unprecedented depth, diversity, and dynamism.

Looking ahead, the integration of AI in creative endeavors opens a window to a future where the act of creation is more accessible, inclusive, and boundless. As we transition from exploring the narrative realms AI helps us traverse, our next focus will shift towards understanding how this technology is influencing other facets of human creativity and interaction, promising an expansion of horizons yet to be fully realized.

Exercise: AI-Assisted Storytelling Session

Objective: Engage with AI-powered writing tools to craft unique stories, exploring new dimensions of narrative creation.

Instructions:

1. **Choose a Writing Assistant:** Select a generative AI tool like Sudowrite or ShortlyAI designed to aid in the writing process.
2. **Start Your Story:** Begin a narrative and use the AI to suggest developments, plot twists, dialogues, or character descriptions.
3. **Shape the Narrative:** Continuously interact with the AI to expand your story, using its suggestions to explore new directions or deepen the narrative.
4. **Reflect and Share:** Analyze how the AI influenced the storytelling process. Share your story or excerpts and your experience using

the AI tool in a writer's group or forum, discussing the blend of human and AI creativity.

Exercise: Interactive Fiction Exploration

Objective: Dive into the world of AI-driven interactive fiction, experiencing firsthand the evolving world of storytelling.

Instructions:

1. **Engage with an Interactive Platform:** Use an AI-driven platform like AI Dungeon to create or participate in an interactive story.
2. **Guide the Story:** Make choices that influence the direction of the narrative, noting how the AI responds and adapts to your decisions.
3. **Document Your Journey:** Keep a log of the key plot points, your decisions, and the AI's contributions to the storytelling.
4. **Analyze and Discuss:** Reflect on the narrative experience, focusing on the AI's role in shaping the story. Discuss the potential of AI in creating personalized and dynamic narratives, and consider the implications for the future of storytelling.

Key Takeaways

- **Collaborate with AI in Music:** Engage with AI music platforms to compose and produce original music, exploring new realms of creativity and expanding your artistic boundaries.
- **Experiment with AI in Visual Arts:** Utilize generative AI tools to create visual artwork, challenging conventional artistic processes and embracing innovative expressions of creativity.
- **Enhance Storytelling with AI:** Leverage AI-assisted writing tools to enrich your storytelling, using AI suggestions to overcome writer's block and add depth to your narratives.

- **Explore Interactive AI Narratives:** Immerse yourself in interactive fiction platforms powered by AI, experiencing dynamic storytelling that adapts to your choices and showcases the potential of AI in reshaping narrative experiences.

Chapter 8

Charting the Course: AI and the Ethical Compass

In a world teeming with technological marvels, AI stands out, sparking both wonder and wariness. From smart assistants in our homes to algorithms that shape our online experiences, AI's influence is undeniable. Yet, as its capabilities grow, so does the importance of guiding this powerful force with a strong moral compass. This chapter delves into the critical balance between innovation and integrity, ensuring AI serves as a force for good.

Balancing Innovation with Integrity

The excitement surrounding what AI can achieve is often tinged with caution, reminding us that without ethical guardrails, technology's potential can veer off course. It's a dance between pushing boundaries and respecting limits, ensuring AI enriches lives without compromising our principles.

Leading by Example: Ethical Oversight in Action

DeepMind, a trailblazer in AI research, has established an ethics board to navigate the morality of its projects. This board isn't just a ceremonial gesture; it plays a pivotal role in steering DeepMind's work, ensuring each innovation aligns with ethical standards. It's a powerful statement: progress doesn't have to come at the expense of principles.

The IEEE, a leading authority in technology standards, has laid down ethical guidelines for AI development. These guidelines serve as a roadmap for creating AI that respects human rights, promotes transparency, and avoids bias. It's like having a moral compass for the digital age, one that points towards technology that respects and uplifts humanity.

The Partnership on AI, bringing together giants like Google and Microsoft, underscores the industry's commitment to ethical standards. This collaboration is not just about sharing best practices; it's a collective effort to shape the future of AI in a way that benefits all of society. It's a testament to the power of unity in forging a technology that is responsible, transparent, and inclusive.

Prioritizing Privacy in the AI Era

In the digital age, privacy has emerged as a cornerstone of ethical technology. **The European Union's General Data Protection Regulation (GDPR)** has set a high bar for how personal data should be handled, emphasizing consent and clarity. It's a robust framework that ensures individuals' rights are front and center, serving as a model for privacy laws worldwide.

Apple's approach to differential privacy demonstrates how technology can harness data while safeguarding privacy. By anonymizing user data, Apple ensures its AI systems can learn and improve without compromising individual privacy. It's a delicate balance, striking the right chord between leveraging data for innovation and respecting the privacy that is fundamental to trust.

Crafting Fairer Futures: Tackling Bias Head-On

The data that feeds AI systems can reflect societal biases, leading to prejudiced outcomes. The **Algorithmic Justice League** shines a spotlight on this issue, advocating for the use of diverse datasets to train AI systems. It's a call to action, urging developers to consider the broader impact of their work and strive for algorithms that are as inclusive as they are innovative.

IBM's Diversity in Faces dataset is a step towards more inclusive AI, providing a varied dataset for facial recognition software. By incorporating a wide range of human faces, IBM aims to reduce bias in AI systems, ensuring technology recognizes and respects our differences. This approach enhances AI's accuracy, fairness, and inclusivity.

AI's Social Contract: Safety, Transparency, and Accountability

In the ever-expanding universe of AI, the concepts of safety, transparency, and accountability act as the North Star, guiding both creators and users toward a future where technology not only empowers but also protects. It's within this framework that we find the true promise of AI—not just in its ability to enhance our lives but in its capacity to do so responsibly.

Navigating the Terrain of AI Safety

Safety in the realm of AI is comparable to the rules governing our roads. They exist to protect individuals, direct them, and ensure a harmonious coexistence of all travelers. In the digital world, this translates to developing algorithms and systems that prevent harm, safeguard privacy, and uphold the dignity of all individuals. The creation of such digital bylaws requires a collaborative effort from all stakeholders, including developers, users, and regulators, to establish an ecosystem where innovation thrives within ethical boundaries.

Regulatory frameworks are crucial, just like traffic laws designed for public safety. Clear regulations for AI development and deployment guide developers in creating technologies that uphold ethical standards, while also providing users with assurance that the AI systems they interact with are designed with their safety in mind.

Risk assessment protocols are in place to ensure an AI system undergoes rigorous testing before deployment, much like a vehicle before it's deemed roadworthy. These assessments evaluate the potential risks and ensure that safeguards are in place to prevent unintended consequences.

Illuminating the Path with Transparency

Transparency is a crucial aspect of AI as it helps users understand how algorithms work and build trust in the technology. When users are aware of how AI systems make decisions, the technology becomes more transparent and easier to comprehend, rather than being viewed as a mysterious black box. This transparency is essential not only for building confidence in AI technologies, but also for creating an informed user base that can engage with AI in meaningful ways.

Initiatives aimed at demystifying AI algorithms, such as public insight into AI decisions, help users gain a clearer perspective on the role technology plays in shaping their digital experiences. By providing insights into the decision-making processes of AI systems, users can better understand how technology impacts their lives.

Efforts like Google's Explainable AI (XAI) strive to bridge the gap between AI complexity and user comprehension. By making AI decisions more understandable, XAI ensures that users and developers alike can better engage with the technology, fostering a collaborative environment where innovation and ethical considerations go hand in hand.

The Cornerstone of Accountability

At the heart of AI's social contract lies accountability. It's the principle that ensures creators and operators of AI systems are answerable for their technology's impact, whether positive or negative. This accountability is crucial for maintaining public trust and fostering an environment where innovation is matched by responsibility.

To ensure AI systems are used safely:

- **Preventive Measures**: Implementing safeguards against misuse from the outset is akin to installing airbags and seatbelts in vehicles. These measures are designed to mitigate risks and protect users from potential harm, emphasizing the importance of foresight in AI development.
- **Learning from Past Mistakes**: The AI Incident Database serves as a collective memory, cataloging instances where AI systems did not perform as intended. This resource is invaluable for researchers and developers, offering lessons learned from previous challenges and guiding future development towards safer, more reliable systems.

In the intricate dance between advancing technology and upholding ethical standards, safety, transparency, and accountability emerge as the guiding principles. They remind us that the path to a future enriched by AI is paved with more than just innovation; it's built on the foundation of trust, understanding, and responsibility. As we navigate this terrain, these principles light the way, ensuring that our journey with AI leads to a destination where technology serves humanity with integrity and respect.

Ethical Design: From Theory to Practice

When crafting the future of AI, integrating ethical considerations from the start isn't just a nod to good manners in innovation; it's critical for creating technology that sustains progress and aligns with our shared values. This proactive approach ensures that as AI systems become more integral to our daily lives, they do so in a way that enhances, rather than detracts from, human dignity and equality.

Integrating Human Values in AI Development

The concept of "value-sensitive design" stands as a beacon for AI developers, guiding them to weave human values into the fabric of technology. This approach prompts a shift in perspective, encouraging creators to view AI systems not just as tools but as entities that interact with and impact people's lives in significant ways. By considering the potential social implications of AI during the design process, developers can create technology that respects human dignity and fosters a more equitable society. "Value-Sensitive Design" is a methodology that imbues AI development with a deep consideration for human values, ensuring that technology enhances rather than undermines the fabric of society. This approach encourages developers to anticipate and mitigate potential negative impacts of AI, paving the way for technology that supports and uplifts marginalized communities.

Championing Social Equity Through Design

The Design Justice Network, in advocating for AI that serves the needs of marginalized communities, highlights the power of technology to bridge divides rather than deepen them. By prioritizing the voices and needs of those often left on the fringes of technological advancement, AI can become a tool for social equity, breaking down barriers and opening doors to new opportunities for all.

The Design Justice Network provides a framework for developing technology that champions inclusivity, ensuring AI products are accessible and beneficial to all segments of society.

Learning from Ethical AI Pioneers

Companies like Salesforce have become trailblazers in ethical AI by establishing offices dedicated to ensuring their AI technologies are developed and deployed with human values at the forefront. Salesforce's Office of Ethical and Humane Use serves as a model, demonstrating how integrating ethical practices into business strategies and product development can lead to more responsible and beneficial AI.

Salesforce's commitment to ethical technology showcases how companies can lead by example, embedding ethics into the very core of their business practices and product designs.

The United Nations' AI for Good initiative exemplifies how AI can be harnessed to tackle some of the most pressing global challenges. By designing AI with ethical intentions and focusing on positive outcomes, this initiative demonstrates the transformative potential of technology to address issues from healthcare to environmental sustainability.

The AI for Good initiative by the United Nations leverages the power of AI to contribute to the betterment of society, showcasing the positive impact of ethically designed technology on global challenges.

Fostering a Culture of Responsibility

To navigate the complexities of AI development responsibly, clear ethical guidelines are essential. The Asilomar AI Principles and The Montreal Declaration for a Responsible Development of Artificial Intelligence serve as compasses, offering developers and users alike a set of guidelines that promote the safe and beneficial development of AI.

These guidelines present frameworks that encourage developers to consider the broader implications of their work, fostering a culture of responsibility within the AI community.

This focus on ethical design, from theory to practice, is more than just a chapter in AI's story; it's a commitment to ensuring technology's immense capabilities are harnessed for the greater good. By embedding values of equity, transparency, and accountability into the very blueprint of AI, we lay the groundwork for a future where technology reflects our highest aspirations for society.

As we wrap up this exploration of ethical AI design, we're reminded that the choices made today in the development and deployment of AI will shape our collective tomorrow. The integration of human values, the championing of social equity, and the adherence to clear ethical guidelines stand as pillars for creating technology that respects and enhances human dignity. Moving forward, the dialogue around AI continues to evolve, inviting us to consider not just the ethical dimensions of technology but also the innovative potential of AI to redefine the boundaries of possibility.

Exercise: Ethical AI Personal Reflection

This quick exercise aims to heighten your awareness of the ethical implications of everyday AI usage, encouraging a mindful approach to technology interactions.

Objective: Reflect briefly on your interaction with AI technology, focusing on ethical considerations.

Instructions:

1. **Identify an AI Interaction:** Think of a recent or common interaction you have with AI technology, like using a smart device, social media algorithms, or online recommendation systems.
2. **Consider Ethical Aspects:** Reflect on two key questions: How does this AI respect your privacy or expose you to potential data risks? Do you perceive this AI as fair and unbiased, or could it potentially discriminate against certain users?
3. **Personal Insight:** Write a few sentences summarizing your thoughts and whether this reflection might influence how you use AI technologies in the future.

Key Takeaways

- **Implement Ethical Frameworks:** Adopt and integrate established ethical guidelines and frameworks into your AI projects to ensure they align with global standards for fairness, transparency, and accountability.
- **Prioritize Data Privacy and Bias Mitigation:** Actively engage in responsible data collection, ensuring privacy protection and implementing measures to identify and reduce biases within AI systems to prevent discriminatory outcomes.

- **Foster Transparency and Accountability:** Develop AI systems with explainable processes and outcomes, ensuring that the technology remains understandable and developers are accountable for their creations.
- **Incorporate Ethical Design Principles:** Embed ethical considerations into the AI development lifecycle, from initial design to deployment, to create technology that not only innovates but also contributes positively to societal well-being.

Chapter 9
AI Tomorrow - Trends Shaping Our Future

Imagine waking up to a world where your coffee machine knows exactly when you need your morning boost or a virtual assistant that not only manages your schedule but also predicts your needs, tweaking your daily routine for optimal productivity and well-being. This scenario isn't ripped from the pages of a science fiction novel. It's the not-so-distant future AI is crafting right before our eyes. From healthcare innovations that spot diseases earlier than ever to financial tools making investment advice accessible to all, AI is touching every facet of our lives, promising a tomorrow that's not only smarter but also more empathetic and inclusive.

The Pulse of Innovation: AI Trends to Watch

AI in Healthcare: A Lifesaver in Your Pocket

Tools are now being developed that can analyze medical images with more precision than the human eye, spotting signs of diseases such as cancer in their infancy when they're most treatable. Imagine an app on your phone that monitors your health, alerting you to see a doctor when something seems off, potentially saving lives with early detection.

The days of one-size-fits-all medicine are numbered. AI is paving the way for treatments tailored to individual genetic profiles, optimizing the effectiveness of healthcare interventions and minimizing side effects. This means that in the near future, the pills you take could be designed specifically for your body's unique needs.

AI in Finance: Your Personal Investment Advisor

Investing can be intimidating, especially for novices. AI-driven robo-advisors are changing the game, offering personalized investment advice at a fraction of the cost of human financial advisors. These platforms can analyze vast amounts of market data in real-time, making recommendations based on your financial goals and risk tolerance.

AI algorithms are becoming increasingly adept at spotting unusual patterns in financial transactions that could indicate fraud. This means safer transactions and lower chances of financial loss due to scams or identity theft, giving you peace of mind every time you check your bank account.

AI in Education: Customized Learning Experiences

AI can adapt educational content to fit the learning pace and style of each student, making education more effective and enjoyable. Picture a virtual tutor that knows just when you're struggling with a concept and can offer additional resources or a new explanation to help you understand.

Teachers spend countless hours grading assignments. AI is set to lighten this load by accurately grading papers and exams, freeing up educators to focus more on teaching and less on administrative tasks. This shift could lead to more dynamic, interactive classroom experiences, with teachers having more time to engage with students on a personal level.

Staying Ahead: Leveraging AI Trends

Keeping up with AI advancements ensures you're not left behind as the technology becomes mainstream. Here's how:

- **Subscribe to AI-focused Publications**: Staying informed is easier when you have sources like 'MIT Technology Review' delivering the latest AI news straight to your inbox. These publications offer insights into current trends and future predictions, giving you a glimpse into how AI might evolve.
- **Attend Industry Conferences**: Events like 'The AI Summit' gather minds from across the globe to discuss AI's trajectory. These gatherings are goldmines for learning about groundbreaking innovations and networking with professionals who are as passionate about AI as you are.
- **Join Online Communities**: Platforms like 'Reddit's r/MachineLearning' bring together AI enthusiasts to share projects, ideas, and challenges. Engaging in these communities can provide support, inspiration, and a sense of belonging in the world of AI.

Ethical AI: The Path Forward

The rise of ethical AI is shaping a future where technology aligns with human values. With sectors like lending and hiring increasingly relying on AI, the demand for transparency in AI's decision-making processes is growing. Tools like 'IBM's Fairness 360 Kit' help developers detect and mitigate bias in their AI models, ensuring decisions are fair and unbiased.

Initiatives like 'Partnership on AI' bring together major tech companies to establish ethical guidelines for AI development and use. These efforts aim to ensure AI benefits society as a whole, prioritizing fairness, inclusivity, and well-being.

As AI continues to weave its way into the fabric of our lives, staying attuned to its evolution is crucial. From breakthroughs that promise to redefine healthcare and finance to innovations ensuring our educational systems are more inclusive and personalized, AI holds the key to a future brimming with possibilities. Balancing this technological prowess with a steadfast commitment to ethics ensures that our journey with AI leads to a destination where technology amplifies our humanity, making our world not just smarter, but also kinder and more equitable.

AI for the Eco-Conscious: Sustainability and AI

The tapestry of modern technology is interwoven with threads of artificial intelligence, each strand promising to revolutionize not just how we interact with machines, but also how we approach the pressing environmental challenges of our times. Amidst growing concerns over climate change and resource depletion, AI emerges not merely as a beacon of innovation but as a vital ally in the quest for sustainability. Its applications span from optimizing energy use to enhancing agricultural practices and conserving the planet's biodiversity, painting a picture of a future where technology and ecology exist in harmony.

Transforming Energy Consumption with AI

A standout example of AI's prowess in driving sustainability is found in the collaborative efforts of DeepMind and Google. Together, they embarked on an initiative to slash energy consumption within Google's data centers, which are notoriously power-hungry facilities. By applying DeepMind's machine learning algorithms to manage cooling systems more efficiently, they achieved a staggering 40% reduction in energy used for cooling. This initiative not only demonstrates the tangible impact of AI on energy conservation but also sets a precedent for how businesses can significantly reduce their carbon footprint with smart technology.

Revolutionizing Agriculture with Precision Farming

The agricultural sector, while being the backbone of global food supply, is also a significant consumer of water and other resources. AI-driven precision farming techniques are turning the tide, making agriculture smarter and more sustainable. By leveraging data on soil conditions, weather patterns, and crop health, AI enables farmers to make informed decisions that optimize resource use and boost yields. This approach not only addresses the challenge of feeding a growing population but does so in a way that minimizes environmental impact.

Preserving Wildlife with AI

In the fight against biodiversity loss, AI is proving to be an invaluable tool. Projects focused on monitoring endangered species and tracking poachers are gaining momentum, harnessing AI to analyze data from camera traps, drones, and satellite imagery. This technology is not just enhancing our understanding of wildlife populations but is also bolstering conservation efforts, making it possible to respond quickly to threats and protect vulnerable species.

Inspiring Greener Career Paths

The growing influence of AI in sustainability opens new avenues for professionals passionate about making a difference. The clean tech industry, in particular, is ripe with opportunities for those eager to explore how AI can be harnessed to address environmental issues. From developing algorithms that predict and mitigate pollution to designing systems that manage renewable energy sources, the potential for impact is limitless.

Similarly, governmental agencies are increasingly looking towards AI to inform and implement policies on sustainable practices. By analyzing environmental data, AI can help shape regulations that protect natural resources and promote green initiatives, offering a path for those interested in bridging technology and policy.

AI's Role in Climate Action

At the heart of AI's contribution to sustainability is its unmatched ability to sift through and make sense of vast amounts of data. In the context of climate change, this capability becomes crucial. AI algorithms are adept at identifying patterns in climate data, predicting shifts in weather patterns, and assessing the impact of human activities on the environment. This information is vital for developing strategies to mitigate climate change and adapt to its effects, positioning AI as a key player in global efforts to safeguard our planet.

Among the innovators leading the charge is Pachama, a company that utilizes AI to monitor forest carbon capture and support reforestation projects. By analyzing satellite imagery, Pachama's AI can assess the health of forests and the effectiveness of reforestation efforts, providing a scalable solution to one of the most pressing challenges of our time—carbon sequestration.

As we navigate the complexities of the 21st century, AI stands not just as a hallmark of human ingenuity but as a testament to our capacity to innovate in harmony with the natural world. Its applications in sustainability offer a glimpse into a future where technology serves as a steward of the planet, ensuring that as we advance, we do so with mindfulness and respect for the environment that sustains us.

Bridging the Skills Gap: AI and Continuing Education

The digital terrain is evolving at an unprecedented pace, driven largely by advancements in artificial intelligence. This rapid growth has significantly influenced job markets, making it clear that acquiring AI skills is no longer a luxury but a necessity for professional development and growth. To stay relevant and competitive, professionals and enthusiasts alike must adopt a mindset of continuous learning.

Platforms Elevating AI Skills

In the quest for AI proficiency, online learning platforms such as Coursera and edX have emerged as invaluable allies. These platforms offer a wide array of courses, ranging from introductory lessons in AI to advanced machine learning techniques. Developed by leading universities and tech giants, the courses are designed to provide both the theoretical foundations and practical applications of AI, making complex concepts accessible to a broad audience.

The beauty of these platforms lies in their flexibility, allowing learners to tailor their education to their schedules and learning pace. For professionals looking to pivot to AI-focused roles, these courses offer a structured path to gaining the necessary skills.

The Value of Continuous Learning and Certifications

In the fast-evolving field of AI, staying updated with the latest technologies and methodologies is crucial. Continuous learning through platforms like Coursera and edX ensures that individuals can keep pace with new developments. Beyond personal enrichment, these platforms offer certifications and micro-credentials in AI, providing verifiable proof of expertise that can be a significant asset in the job market.

Preparing the Next Generation

As AI becomes more embedded in our daily lives, introducing its concepts to children prepares them for a future where technology and daily life are inextricably linked. Programs like Code.org play a crucial role in this preparation, offering resources that make learning about AI engaging and accessible.

Corporate training programs are also recognizing the importance of AI literacy, integrating AI courses into their development programs. For example, Amazon's Machine Learning University, initially developed to train Amazon's developers in machine learning, has expanded its reach, offering its courses to the public. This move underscores the growing recognition of AI's impact across all sectors and the need for a workforce skilled in these technologies.

Transitioning to an AI-Focused Career

For many, the question remains: "How do I transition into an AI-related career?" The answer lies in a clear, step-by-step approach that begins with foundational knowledge and progressively builds up to specialized skills.

1. **Start with the Basics**: Enroll in introductory courses on Coursera or edX to gain a solid understanding of AI principles.
2. **Build Upon Foundation**: Once comfortable with the basics, tackle more advanced courses to deepen your understanding and learn about specific AI applications relevant to your field.
3. **Practical Experience**: Engage in hands-on projects available on platforms like Kaggle, which provide real-world problems for you to solve using AI, reinforcing your learning and building your portfolio.
4. **Seek Mentorship**: Platforms like MentorCruise offer opportunities to connect with experienced professionals in AI who can provide guidance, feedback, and support as you navigate your career transition.
5. **Earn Certifications and Digital Badges**: Completing courses and earning certifications not only validates your skills but also signals your commitment to professional development to potential employers.

Inspiring Success Stories

The path to an AI-centric career is unique for everyone but understanding the journeys of those who have successfully made the transition can offer valuable insights. From software developers who've pivoted to machine learning roles to marketers leveraging AI to enhance customer engagement strategies, the applications of AI are wide and varied. These success stories underscore the transformative power of AI education and the opportunities it opens up across industries.

Professionals offering mentorship through platforms like MentorCruise often share their experiences, providing not just technical guidance but also inspiration. Their journeys highlight the versatility of AI education and its potential to propel careers in new, exciting directions.

In an era where AI's influence on the job market is undeniable, embracing continuous learning and seeking opportunities to upskill are pivotal.

Whether you're a seasoned professional eyeing a career shift or a curious learner starting your journey, the resources and pathways to mastering AI are more accessible than ever. As we navigate this, the blend of online courses, practical projects, and mentorship offers a comprehensive approach to not just learning about AI but truly integrating it into our professional lives, ensuring we remain at the forefront of technological innovation and advancement.

Cultivating AI Literacy: Resources and Tools for Beginners

Navigating the enormous amount of information on artificial intelligence can feel like trying to find a lighthouse in a storm for those just starting out. Yet, the exact resources can turn this seemingly daunting voyage into a smooth sail. Here's a guide to the lighthouses - resources and tools that illuminate the path for beginners in AI.

Kaggle stands out as an invaluable resource for hands-on learning. It's a platform where beginners can dive into practical data science projects, offering a chance to apply theoretical knowledge to real-world problems. Kaggle competitions provide a unique opportunity to test your skills against a global community, offering both a challenge and a learning experience.

For those who prefer learning on the go, podcasts offer a gateway to the world of AI. 'AI in Business' is a podcast that demystifies AI concepts, breaking them down into digestible insights perfect for a commute or workout. It brings experts into your ears, offering perspectives on how AI is transforming industries.

DataCamp offers a hands-on approach to learning AI, with coding challenges designed specifically for newcomers. These interactive exercises guide you through the basics of programming and data analysis, offering immediate feedback and the satisfaction of seeing your code come to life.

Visual programming tools like Scratch introduce the logic behind AI and programming without the need for advanced coding skills. It's an environment where you can experiment, create, and learn through doing, making it an excellent starting point for beginners.

Simulation environments such as AnyLogic provide a sandbox for modeling complex systems with AI. These tools offer a glimpse into the power of AI in understanding and predicting the behavior of systems, from logistics to human dynamics, all without writing a single line of code.

Starting with AI doesn't have to be a leap into the unknown. Begin by exploring AI's impact on an area that sparks your curiosity. This personal connection can serve as a powerful motivator, making the learning process more engaging and relevant.

Setting achievable goals, like completing a specific AI project or course within six months, can help maintain momentum. These milestones provide a sense of progression and accomplishment, fueling your desire to learn more.

Joining study groups or online forums, such as Stack Overflow, invites collaboration and support. These communities offer a space to ask questions, share discoveries, and learn from the experiences of others, making the journey into AI a shared adventure.

As we wrap up this exploration of resources and tools for cultivating AI literacy, it's clear that a world of opportunity awaits those willing to dive in. From Kaggle's practical challenges to the engaging insights of AI podcasts, and the interactive learning experiences offered by DataCamp, there's a wealth of resources designed to guide beginners from novice to knowledgeable. Visual programming tools and simulation environments further demystify AI, making it accessible to all. By starting with a curiosity-driven approach, setting clear goals, and embracing the support of online communities, anyone can embark on a fulfilling journey into the realm of AI.

These stepping stones not only equip you with the knowledge and skills to navigate the AI world but also open doors to new possibilities, where AI's transformative power can be harnessed to innovate, create, and solve the challenges of tomorrow. As we look ahead, the journey continues, promising new horizons and opportunities to shape the future with AI.

Exercise: AI Trend Exploration

Objective: Quickly identify and explore a current AI trend to understand its impact and potential applications.

Instructions:

1. **Research Current AI Trends:** Spend 5 minutes online to identify one emerging AI trend that interests you. This could be a new technology, application, or innovation in any field such as healthcare, finance, or sustainability.
2. **Summarize the Trend:** Write a brief summary (2-3 sentences) explaining the trend and why it caught your attention.
3. **Reflect on Impact:** Consider the potential implications of this trend. In a few sentences, describe how it might affect an industry, change a daily task, or influence societal practices.
4. **Personal Relevance:** Quickly jot down any ideas on how this trend could be relevant to your personal or professional life, or how you might adapt to or embrace this innovation.

Key Takeaways

- **Monitor AI Trends:** Regularly update yourself on AI developments to stay current and informed.
- **Embrace AI for Green Initiatives:** Utilize AI to support and enhance environmental sustainability efforts.
- **Prioritize AI Learning:** Continuously upgrade your AI skills through online courses and certifications.

- **Prepare for AI's Future:** Strategically anticipate and adapt to the evolving impact of AI on various sectors.
- **Improve Your AI Literacy:** Leverage diverse, beginner-friendly AI resources like Kaggle, DataCamp, and AI podcasts to quickly transition from novice to proficient in AI.

Chapter 10

Mastering the AI Terrain:
Your Blueprint for Success

Picture a world where each of us has a digital twin, an AI companion tuned perfectly to our learning habits, professional ambitions, and personal interests. This isn't just a thought experiment—it's a very real possibility in the near future. But before we get there, we need to chart our path through the evolving topography of artificial intelligence, picking up the right tools, knowledge, and connections along the way.

The starting point is crafting your personal AI roadmap, a tailored guide that aligns with your goals, whether it's to create a voice-activated assistant, analyze huge datasets, or simply understand the AI that permeates our daily lives. This chapter breaks down how to construct this plan, ensuring you're well-equipped for the journey ahead.

Your Personal AI Roadmap: Setting the Stage for Success

Identify Your AI Interests and Goals

Start with a self-assessment to pinpoint exactly what draws you to AI. Is it the allure of building intelligent systems, or perhaps the promise of data-driven insights that can transform businesses? Once you have a clear picture, outline your goals. Maybe you're aiming to build a chatbot by the year's end or become proficient in Python to analyze data. Knowing where you want to head is the first step in plotting your course.

Craft a Learning Plan Tailored to Your Interests

Platforms like LinkedIn Learning are treasure troves of AI knowledge, offering courses that range from beginner to advanced levels. Dive into these resources with your goals in mind. For instance, if data analytics piques your interest, start with foundational courses in data science before moving on to more specialized AI training.

Set achievable milestones along your learning path. Celebrating small victories, like completing a Python course or building a basic neural network, can boost your morale and keep you motivated.

Stay Inspired and Informed

AI is a field that's constantly evolving, and staying updated can be as inspiring as it is informative. Following influencers like Fei-Fei Li and Andrew Ng on social media platforms gives you a window into the latest breakthroughs and ongoing debates in the AI world. Their insights can spark new ideas and offer perspectives on where AI is headed next.

Subscribe to newsletters like 'The Algorithm' by MIT Technology Review or 'Import AI' by Jack Clark. These weekly digests serve up fresh developments, thoughtful analyses, and forecasts about AI's trajectory, ensuring you're never out of the loop.

Engage with online communities such as Data Science Central or the AI and Data Science Community on LinkedIn. These forums are where peers, novices, and experts alike share resources, discuss trends, and solve problems together—a great way to deepen your understanding and connect with like-minded individuals.

Make Continuous Learning a Habit

Allocate a set number of hours each week to your AI education. This could involve reading the latest articles, tackling quizzes, or experimenting with AI tools. It's this regular commitment that transforms sporadic interest into solid expertise.

Apps like Habitica can make learning more engaging by turning it into a game where you earn rewards for hitting your study goals. This approach adds a layer of fun to the process, making it less of a chore and more of an adventure.

Don't miss out on virtual meetups and webinars hosted by AI organizations. These events not only provide valuable learning opportunities but also help you stay connected with the AI community, offering a platform to learn from others' experiences and share your own.

The following checklist serves as a quick reference to keep your learning journey on track, ensuring you're covering all bases as you navigate the world of AI.

AI LEARNING *checklist*

- ☐ **IDENTIFY AI INTERESTS AND SPECIFIC GOALS**
- ☐ SELECT BEGINNER-FRIENDLY COURSES ON LINKEDIN LEARNING
- ☐ **SET REALISTIC MILESTONES AND CELEBRATE ACHIEVING THEM**
- ☐ FOLLOW AI INFLUENCERS ON SOCIAL MEDIA AND SUBSCRIBE TO AI-FOCUSED NEWSLETTERS
- ☐ **DEDICATE WEEKLY HOURS TO LEARNING AND EXPERIMENTING WITH AI**
- ☐ GAMIFY LEARNING EXPERIENCE WITH APPS LIKE HABITICA
- ☐ **PARTICIPATE IN VIRTUAL MEETUPS AND WEBINARS**

ModernMind Publications

Crafting your personal AI roadmap is much like preparing for a voyage into uncharted territories. With the right plan in place, you're not just wandering; you're exploring with purpose. This blueprint, tailored to your interests and ambitions, ensures that each step you take brings you closer to your goals in the realm of artificial intelligence. Whether you're drawn to the promise of big data, the allure of machine learning, or the challenge of creating intelligent systems, this roadmap is your guide to turning aspirations into achievements in the field of AI.

Bridging Theory with Practice: From Concepts to Real-World AI

Diving into the world of artificial intelligence, it soon becomes clear that the leap from understanding its principles to applying them in tangible projects is where true learning blossoms. This phase is about rolling up your sleeves and turning your acquired knowledge into action. Here's how to make that pivot, moving from absorbing information to creating with AI.

Hands-On Experience with DIY Projects

Imagine transforming your living space into an ecosystem of smart devices, all built by you. Engaging with platforms like Raspberry Pi opens up a playground for such innovation. Here's where you can start:

- **Weather Station**: By assembling a Raspberry Pi weather station, you fine-tune your coding skills and learn to process environmental data. This project not only sharpens your technical abilities but also gives you insights into data analysis, making sense of temperature, humidity, and air pressure readings.
- **Motion-Detecting Security Camera**: Crafting a security camera that alerts you to movement introduces you to the intersection of hardware and software. It's a practical way to delve into computer vision, one of AI's most exciting fields, teaching you to interpret and act upon visual data.

Competitive Spirit on Online Platforms

Nothing tests your skills quite like competition. Platforms such as DrivenData and Zindi host challenges that address real-world issues, from climate change to public health, offering a unique opportunity to apply AI for social good. Here's why participating is worthwhile:

- **Global Challenges**: Competing in these contests pits you against a global community, exposing you to diverse approaches and solutions. It's a learning experience that broadens your perspective, pushing you to refine your approach to problem-solving.

- **Practical Impact**: These competitions often revolve around pressing societal issues, giving your work a purpose beyond the technical challenge. It's rewarding to see your AI solutions potentially making a difference in the world.

Experimentation with Google Colab

Google Colab simplifies the process of experimenting with AI, offering a cloud-based platform where you can write and execute Python code. Its convenience and accessibility make it an ideal tool.

- **Code and Dataset Experimentation**: With Google Colab, you have the freedom to test various algorithms and datasets without worrying about your computer's processing capabilities. It's an excellent way to see immediate results from your code changes, aiding your understanding of AI's dynamics.
- **System Mechanics**: The platform serves as a practical introduction to the mechanics behind AI systems. You learn to troubleshoot, iterate, and improve your models, gaining a deeper appreciation for the intricacies of AI development.

Collaborating with Local Organizations

AI has the power to transform communities. By collaborating with local businesses and nonprofits, you can contribute meaningful solutions while honing your skills. Consider these possibilities:

- **Sales Data Analysis for a Bookstore**: Dive into the sales data of a neighborhood bookstore, using AI to unearth patterns that can optimize inventory and boost sales. This project not only benefits the store but also enhances your data analytics skills.

- **AI-Powered Recommendation System**: A community center could greatly benefit from an AI system that recommends resources and workshops based on visitors' interests. Such a project allows you to explore recommendation algorithms, a cornerstone of AI applications.
- **Social Media Strategy for Non-Profits**: Crafting an AI-driven strategy to enhance a non-profit's social media outreach teaches you about natural language processing and sentiment analysis, crucial for understanding and engaging online communities effectively.

Sharing Your AI Journey

Documenting and sharing your AI projects not only builds your portfolio but also invites feedback that can propel your growth. Here's how to go about it:

- **Blogging on Platforms Like Medium**: A blog allows you to narrate your AI adventures, detailing the challenges you faced and how you overcame them. It's a reflective practice that solidifies your learning and inspires others.
- **Vlogging on YouTube**: Creating video content about your projects offers a dynamic way to showcase your work, providing insights into your thought process and the practical steps involved in your projects.
- **GitHub for Collaboration**: Sharing your projects on GitHub not only serves as a record of your accomplishments but also opens up opportunities for collaboration. It's a platform where feedback can lead to refinement and innovation.
- **Presentations at Local Meetups**: Taking the stage at tech meetups or school events to present your projects sharpens your public speaking skills. It's a chance to articulate your vision, receive direct feedback, and connect with potential collaborators.

Through these activities, the journey from learning AI concepts to applying them becomes not just a path of personal growth but a shared adventure. By diving into projects, engaging in competitions, partnering with local entities, and openly sharing your experiences, you bridge the gap between theoretical knowledge and real-world application. This approach not only enhances your understanding of AI but also prepares you for a future where these technologies play a central role in solving complex problems and enhancing everyday life.

Beyond the Basics: Nurturing a Growth Mindset in AI

Exploring AI introduces us to a realm where curiosity fuels advancement and challenges serve as milestones. Venturing into complex concepts such as reinforcement learning or generative adversarial networks might seem daunting at first glance. However, breaking these into smaller, digestible pieces transforms them into intriguing puzzles waiting to be solved.

Platforms like TensorFlow Hub democratize access to cutting-edge AI models. Here, anyone with an internet connection can play around with pre-trained models. It's like having a sandbox where you can manipulate algorithms that professionals and researchers have developed, offering a hands-on way to understand the intricacies of advanced AI.

Diving into case studies, such as Atomwise's use of AI in accelerating drug discovery, illustrates the profound impact of AI. These stories not only highlight AI's potential to solve complex problems but also inspire us to think about how we can apply AI in our own fields of interest.

Creating or joining a study group dedicated to AI propels your learning journey forward. Platforms like Meetup facilitate these connections, allowing you to find or start a local AI group. The value lies in shared learning; challenges that stump you might be a piece of cake for someone else, and vice versa. It's a collective journey where everyone brings something to the table.

Online forums such as Reddit's r/learnmachinelearning serve as a hive of activity. Here, queries bounce around, solutions are shared, and support is just a post away. The camaraderie found in these forums often leads to collaborative projects, further enhancing your learning experience.

Virtual hackathons or study jams present an excellent opportunity to apply your skills. Organizing these with friends or colleagues not only tests your knowledge but also fosters a spirit of teamwork and innovation. It's a dynamic way to see AI concepts come to life, solving problems and creating projects together.

Reflecting on your progress is crucial for growth. Keeping a learning diary or journal helps you track what you've learned, the obstacles you've encountered, and how you've overcome them. It's a personal log that shows how far you've come and where you might need to focus more.

Tools like Trello or Notion offer a structured way to manage your resources and plan your activities. They act as a dashboard for your AI exploration, helping you stay organized and focused on your goals.

Regularly reviewing your progress ensures you're on the right track. Setting aside time every few months to evaluate what's working and what isn't allows you to adjust your strategy, ensuring constant improvement and adaptation.

The realm of AI is seemingly boundless, offering endless opportunities for those willing to explore it. By moving beyond the basics and embracing the complexities of advanced concepts, you unlock new levels of understanding and capability. It's a path that demands curiosity, collaboration, and reflection, but the rewards are immense. Not only do you gain a deeper appreciation for the power of AI, but you also equip yourself with the skills to contribute to its evolution.

As we close this chapter, we're reminded that AI is not just any field of study but one that is filled with opportunity. From the intricacies of machine learning models to the collaborative spirit of study groups, every aspect of AI offers a chance to grow, innovate, and impact the world around us. Looking ahead, the journey into AI continues to unfold, promising new discoveries, challenges, and the chance to shape the future of technology.

Exercise: Crafting Your AI Vision Board

Objective: Create a visual representation of your goals and aspirations in the AI field to serve as a constant source of inspiration and guidance on your learning journey.

Instructions:

1. **Define Your AI Goals:** Reflect on what you want to achieve in the world of AI. Consider career aspirations, skill development, innovative projects, or contributions to societal challenges.
2. **Gather Inspiration:** Collect images, quotes, articles, and any other materials that inspire you or represent your aspirations in AI.
3. **Create Your Board:** Digitally (using a tool like Canva or Pinterest) or on a physical board, arrange your collected items into a cohesive vision board. Include your set goals, inspirational figures, desired projects, and key learning milestones.
4. **Interactive Element:** Incorporate interactive elements such as QR codes linking to online AI resources, tutorials, or communities; or create a section that you can update with stickers or notes as you achieve your milestones.
5. **Placement for Motivation:** Place your vision board in a spot where you will see it daily to keep your AI goals top of mind and draw continuous inspiration.

Key Takeaways

- **Develop a Personal AI Roadmap:** Outline your learning objectives, pinpoint AI topics that excite you, and set achievable milestones to track your progress and celebrate your successes.

- **Engage with Hands-on AI Projects:** Apply your theoretical knowledge to real-world scenarios through DIY AI projects, online competitions, or collaborative initiatives with local organizations.
- **Showcase Your AI Journey:** Document and share your AI projects and experiences, building a portfolio that reflects your skills, insights, and contributions to the field.
- **Cultivate Continuous Learning:** Stay committed to advancing your understanding of AI, embracing complex concepts, participating in community learning, and regularly reflecting on and adjusting your educational path.

Conclusion

As we draw the curtains on this journey from the foundational stones of generative AI to its creative and business implementations, we've navigated through a maze of concepts, applications, and hands-on exercises. Together, we've peeled back layers of complexity to reveal the core of AI, transforming abstract ideas into tangible knowledge and skills. This book was designed not just as a guide but as a companion in demystifying AI, showcasing its real-world applications, and providing you with interactive components to cement your understanding.

Reflecting on the vision that sparked the creation of this book, it was my deepest hope to forge a comprehensive guide that breaks down the barriers to understanding AI for beginners and those not deeply entrenched in technology. The aim was to illuminate the path to AI in a manner that speaks to everyone, regardless of technical prowess, and to empower you to harness AI in shaping your world.

Now, standing at the threshold of this journey's end, I extend a call to action to you. Armed with the insights and knowledge you've gained, I encourage you to leap into creating your AI projects. Let curiosity be your compass as you delve deeper into the realms of AI. Engage with the vibrant community of AI enthusiasts and practitioners to continue expanding your horizons. The journey of learning never truly ends, and every step forward is a step towards mastery and innovation.

Imagine the myriad possibilities that lie ahead as you integrate AI into your life, career, and community. Think of the doors yet to be opened, the solutions waiting to be discovered, and the impact you can create. AI is not just a tool of the future; it is the future—yours to shape and define.

I want to extend my heartfelt thanks to you for embarking on this exploration of generative AI with me. It is my sincere hope that this book has not only enriched your understanding but also kindled a flame of passion for AI within you. Your dedication to learning and growing in this field is the first step towards a future brimming with possibilities.

I welcome and cherish your feedback on this book. Sharing your experiences, insights, and the projects you embark on enriches our collective journey in AI. I invite you to connect with me and the broader AI community through social media, forums, or at AI events and meetups. Together, we can continue to explore, learn, and push the boundaries of what's possible with AI.

Thank you for your time, your curiosity, and your commitment to learning about generative AI. Here's to the endless possibilities that await us in the exciting, evolving world of artificial intelligence.

Let's keep the conversation going, and may our paths cross again in the journey of continuous learning and discovery.

With gratitude and best wishes for your AI adventures,

Lauren
ModernMind Publications

Help Somebody Just Like You

Congratulations! Now that you've unlocked the secrets of Generative AI and ChatGPT, how would you like to help others do the same? Your honest review on Amazon can help guide others by providing the insights they need to understand and use this technology effectively.

Your feedback supports the AI community by enhancing the learning experience and broadening the impact of this book for all readers.

Scan the QR code to leave your review.

Thank you for your crucial role in this journey and for helping to foster innovation and discovery in the AI community.

With gratitude,

ModernMind Publications

References

- *Complete Beginner's Guide to Generative AI* https://www.dreamhost.-com/blog/guide-to-generative-ai/
- *Top Generative AI Industry Applications & Use Cases* https://www.turing.com/re-sources/generative-ai-applications
- *The Difference Between Generative AI And Traditional AI* https://www.forbes.-com/sites/bernardmarr/2023/07/24/the-difference-between-generative-ai-and-traditional-ai-an-easy-explanation-for-anyone/
- *The rise of generative AI: A timeline of breakthrough innovations* https://www.qual-comm.com/news/onq/2024/02/the-rise-of-generative-ai-timeline-of-breakthrough-innovations#:~:text=DALL%2DE%2C%20Midjour-ney%20and%20Stable,level%20of%20detail%20and%20realism.
- *How Generative AI Is Changing Creative Work* https://hbr.org/2022/11/how-generative-ai-is-changing-creative-work
- *Case Studies - Artificial Intelligence for the Music Industry* https://musiio.com/clients
- *Generative AI Ethics: 8 Biggest Concerns and Risks* https://www.techtarget.-com/searchenterpriseai/tip/Generative-AI-ethics-8-biggest-concerns#:~:text=Like%20other%20forms%20of%20AI,copyright%20infringe-ments%20and%20harmful%20content.
- *6 Ways Generative AI is Transforming the Entertainment Industry* https://dasha.ai/en-us/blog/-ways-generative-ai-is-transforming-the-entertainment-industry
- *33 Booming Generative AI Companies & Startups (2024)* https://explodingtopics.-com/blog/generative-ai-startups
- *How Generative AI Is Already Transforming Customer ...* https://www.bcg.com/pub-lications/2023/how-generative-ai-transforms-customer-service
- *10 Generative AI Supply Chain Use Cases in 2024* https://research.aimultiple.-com/generative-ai-supply-chain/
- *Ethics First: The Imperative Of Responsible AI Adoption In Marketing* https://www.forbes.com/sites/sunshinefarzan/2023/09/29/ethics-first-the-imperative-of-responsible-ai-adoption-in-marketing/
- *The 7 best AI courses for beginners* https://zapier.com/blog/best-ai-courses/
- *4 Ways AI is Transforming Community Learning Experience* https://www.grazitti.-com/resource/articles/4-ways-ai-powered-online-learning-communities-are-transforming-learning-experience/

References

- *How to Build Generative AI Model Using Python? [Step-by- ...* https://www.ml-tut.com/how-to-build-generative-ai-model/
- *AI And VR Technology In Education: The Future Of Learning* https://elearningin-dustry.com/evolving-education-the-impact-of-ai-and-vr-technology-on-the-future-of-learning

Also by ModernMind Publications

Check out our other books by scanning the QR code:

Printed in Great Britain
by Amazon

43867270R00079